First Workshop on Natural Language Processing for Internet Freedom (NLP4IF-2018)

Santa Fe, New Mexico, USA
20 August 2018

ISBN: 978-1-5108-6909-7

Printed from e-media with permission by:

Curran Associates, Inc.
57 Morehouse Lane
Red Hook, NY 12571

CURRAN ASSOCIATES INC. proceedings .com

Some format issues inherent in the e-media version may also appear in this print version.

Printed by Curran Associates, Inc. (2018)

Association for Computational Linguistics
209 N. Eighth Street
Stroudsburg, Pennsylvania 18360

Phone: 1-570-476-8006
Fax: 1-570-476-0860

acl@aclweb.org

Additional copies of this publication are available from:

Curran Associates, Inc.
57 Morehouse Lane
Red Hook, NY 12571 USA
Phone: 845-758-0400
Fax: 845-758-2633
Email: curran@proceedings.com
Web: www.proceedings.com

COLING 2018

The 27th International Conference on Computational Linguistics

Proceedings of the First Workshop on Natural Language Processing for Internet Freedom (NLP4IF-2018)

August 20, 2018
Santa Fe, New Mexico, USA

Introduction

Welcome to the First Workshop on NLP for Internet Freedom. Our workshop has been inspired by the recent report produced by Freedom House (freedomhouse.org), an "independent watchdog organization dedicated to the expansion of freedom and democracy around the world", which states that Internet freedom declined in 2016 for the sixth consecutive year. 67% of all Internet users live in countries where criticism of the government, military, or ruling family are subject to censorship. Social media users face unprecedented penalties, as authorities in 38 countries made arrests based on social media posts over the past year. Globally, 27% of all internet users live in countries where people have been arrested for publishing, sharing, or merely "liking" content on Facebook. Governments are increasingly going after messaging apps like WhatsApp and Telegram, which can spread information quickly and securely. Various barriers exist to prevent citizens of a large number of countries to access information. Some involve infrastructural and economic barriers, others violations of user rights such as surveillance, privacy and repercussions for online speech and activities such as imprisonment, extralegal harassment or cyberattacks. Yet another area is limits on content, which involves legal regulations on content, technical filtering and blocking websites, (self-)censorship. Large internet providers are effective monopolies, and themselves have the power to use NLP techniques to control information flow. Users are suspended or banned, sometimes without human intervention, and with little opportunity for redress. Users react to this by using coded, oblique or metaphorical language, by taking steps to conceal their identity such as the use of multiple accounts, raising questions about who the real originating author of a post actually is. This workshop brings together NLP researchers whose work contributes to the free flow of information on the Internet.

The papers in this volume all focus on censorship in China. Heng Ji and Kevin Knight discuss obfuscated language that people often create to avoid Internet censorship. The authors also give an overview of automated techniques needed to simulate human encoding. Knockell et al. conduct an in-depth study of blacklists and their variability across and within domains. Ng et al. discuss the linguistic properties of censored and uncensored social media posts.

Thanks to the US National Science Foundation support (award No. 1828199), we were able to bring in three speakers from the NLP community and beyond. Dr. Jedidiah Crandall (University of New Mexico) will give a talk entitled "How to Talk Dirty and Influence Machines". Dr. Jennifer Pan (Stanford University) will give a talk on how the Chinese government fabricates social media posts for strategic distraction, not engaged argument. Nancy Watzman (Dot Connector Studio) will discuss what journalists really want from NLP researchers and how to help build trust in media and democracy by helping journalists make sense of big data. Finally, we will also hold a panel session on NLP and Disinformation.

Last but not least, we would like to thank the program committee for their help with reviewing the papers, organizing and advertising the workshop.

See you in Santa Fee on August 20!

Chris Brew, Anna Feldman, and Chris Leberknight

Organizers:

Chris Brew
Anna Feldman, Montclair State University
Chris Leberknight, Montclair State University

Program Committee:

Joan Bachenko, Deception Discovery Technologies, NJ, USA
Jedidiah Crandall, University of New Mexico, NM, USA
Chaya Hiruncharoenvate, Mahasarakham University, Thailand
Lifu Huang, Rensselaer Polytechnic Institute (RPI), NY, USA
Zubin Jelveh, The University of Chicago, IL, USA
Judith Klavans, Columbia University, NY, USA
Jeffrey Knockel, University of New Mexico, NM, USA
Will Lowe, Princeton University, NJ, USA
Rada Mihalcea, University of Michigan, Ann Arbor, MI, USA
Prateek Mittal, Princeton University, NJ, USA
Rishab Nithyanand, Data & Society, NY, USA
Noah Smith, University of Washington, WA, USA
Thamar Solorio, University of Houston, TX, USA
Mahmood Sharif, Carnegie Mellon University, PA, USA
Evan Sultanik, Trail of Bits, NY, USA
Svitlana Volkova, Pacific Northwest National Laboratory, WA, USA
Brook Wu, New Jersey Institute of Technology, NJ, USA

Invited Speakers:

Dr. Jedidiah Crandall, University of New Mexico
Dr. Jennifer Pan, Stanford University, CA
Nancy Watzman, Dot Connector Studio

Table of Contents

Conference Program

09:00–10:00 **Invited talk: Jennifer Pan (Stanford University):** ***How the Chinese Government Fabricates Social Media Posts for Strategic Distraction, Not Engaged Argument***

10:00–10:30 *The Effect of Information Controls on Developers in China: An Analysis of Censorship in Chinese Open Source Projects*
Jeffrey Knockel, Masashi Crete-Nishihata and Lotus Ruan

10:30–11:00 **Coffee Break**

11:00–12:00 **Invited talk: Jed Crandall (University of New Mexico):** ***How to Talk Dirty and Influence Machines***

12:00–12:30 *Linguistic Characteristics of Censorable Language on SinaWeibo*
Kei Yin Ng, Anna Feldman, Jing Peng and Chris Leberknight

12:30–02:00 **Lunch**

02:00–03:00 **Invited Talk: Nancy Watzman (Dot Connector Studio):** ***What do Journalists Really Want from NLP Researchers? How to Help Build Trust in Media and Democracy by Helping Journalists Make Sense of Big Data***

03:00–03:30 *Creative Language Encoding under Censorship*
Heng Ji and Kevin Knight

03:30–04:00 **Coffee Break**

04:00–05:00 **Panel: NLP and Disinformation (Moderator: Chris Brew)**

The effect of information controls on developers in China: An analysis of censorship in Chinese open source projects

Jeffrey Knockel, Masashi Crete-Nishihata, and Lotus Ruan
The Citizen Lab, Munk School of Global Affairs, University of Toronto
{jeff,masashi,lotusruan}@citizenlab.ca

Abstract

Censorship of Internet content in China is understood to operate through a system of intermediary liability whereby service providers are liable for the content on their platforms. Previous work studying censorship has found huge variability in the implementation of censorship across different products even within the same industry segment. In this work we explore the extent to which these censorship features are present in the open source projects of individual developers in China by collecting their blacklists and comparing their similarity. We collect files from a popular online code repository, extract lists of strings, and then classify whether each is a Chinese blacklist. Overall, we found over 1,000 Chinese blacklists comprising over 200,000 unique keywords, representing the largest dataset of Chinese blacklisted keywords to date. We found very little keyword overlap between lists, raising questions as to their origins, as the lists seem too large to have been individually curated, yet the lack of overlap suggests that they have no common source.

1 Introduction

Censorship of Internet content in China is conducted through a system of intermediary liability or "self-discipline" in which service providers are held liable for content on their platforms (MacKinnon, 2011). Service providers are expected to invest in technology and personnel to implement content censorship according to government regulations. Previous work has identified content censorship in a range of applications used in the Chinese market including chat apps (Knockel et al., 2011; Crandall et al., 2013; Hardy, 2013; Ruan et al., 2016), live streaming services (Knockel et al., 2015; Crete-Nishihata et al., 2016), blogs (MacKinnon, 2010), microblogs (Bamman et al., 2012; Miller, 2017), search engines (Villeneuve, 2006), and online games (Knockel et al., 2017). These studies found that the system of censorship in China is decentralized and fragmented due in part to the vaguely defined content regulations and multiple lines of authority between private companies and government bodies. This fragmentation leads to significant variability in how censorship is implemented across different products even within the same industry segment.

While the information control pressures on commercial companies operating in China are well understood, the effect of these controls on individual developers is understudied. Do individual developers include censorship features such as keyword filtering lists in their projects? If they do what is their motivation and how do they create the lists? In this paper we work toward understanding how information controls affect individual developers in China by identifying software projects with keyword blacklists on the popular code repository GitHub. The presence of keyword blacklists used to trigger censorship on GitHub projects suggests that developers perceive or experience some level of informal or formal pressure to include censorship features in their projects.

We developed a novel heuristic tool to extract lists of strings from a variety of structured data formats as used in projects hosted on GitHub. We then designed a method for reliably determining whether a list of strings is a sensitive list of Chinese keywords. These techniques resulted in collection of over 1,000

Proceedings of the First Workshop on Natural Language Processing for Internet Freedom, pages 1–11
Santa Fe, New Mexico, USA, August 20, 2018.

keyword blacklists extracted from GitHub projects, which collectively contain hundreds of thousands of unique keywords representing the largest dataset of Chinese keyword blacklists collected to date.

We conclude with discussion of questions to investigate in future research including understanding what motivates the developers to include these keyword lists in their projects and how their blacklists are created. Developers may be concerned that they themselves or others using or deploying their projects may fall under the Chinese regulation of service providers and that they may be held liable for content shared on their applications in a similar way to how commercial companies are regulated. They may also be generally accustomed to censorship requirements for software projects and understand it as necessary for introducing an application to the Chinese market. It may also be that they believe their applications should be censored and share the political concerns that motivate the Chinese government. We propose an interview study with the developers to gain insights into their motivations. The process that developers use to create the lists is also an open question. Given the size of these lists, their origin is unclear, as they seem too large for developers to have individually compiled, yet given the lack of overlap between the lists, it seems they are not coming from common sources either. This finding is similar to analysis of censorship keyword lists extracted from commercial applications used in China, which also found lack of overlap between products and industry segments (Crandall et al., 2013; Knockel et al., 2015; Crete-Nishihata et al., 2016; Knockel et al., 2017). Follow-up qualitative research on the developers and analysis of GitHub commit history may provide us with a better understanding of how the lists are created and shared. Overall, the keyword lists we extracted from developer projects and the open questions they present reveal a further avenue to probe the underlying motivations and processes behind application-based censorship in China.

2 Background

Founded in 2008, GitHub is a globally popular open source software development and sharing platform. As of 2017, GitHub reportedly had 24 million developers working across 67 million repositories (GitHub, 2017). In 2017 alone, 692,000 users from China signed up for an account on GitHub, and nearly one-third of all China-based developers used GitHub (崔绮雯, 2015), many of whom worked for Chinese Internet giants including Baidu, Tencent, and Alibaba (Open Source China, 2016).

GitHub has also been the target of censorship in China. On January 21, 2013, GitHub was blocked in China using DNS hijacking (Protalinski, 2013). While there was no official response from the Chinese government, Chinese users speculated that the blocking was due to GitHub's hosting of plug-in software that allowed purchasing of train tickets before the Spring Festival rush in China, which was discouraged by the Ministry of Railways (雅楠, 2013). On January 23, 2013, GitHub was accessible again in China (Bai Tiantian, 2013).

On January 26, 2013, GitHub's China-based users experienced a MITM attack in which attackers could have intercepted traffic between the site and its users in China. (GreatFire, 2013) The mechanism of the attack was through a fake SSL certificate. The motivations behind this attack were not clear, but it may have been used to collect the passwords of China-based GitHub users. The attack was lifted after about an hour.

On March 26, 2015, the Chinese censorship apparatus employed a new tool, the "Great Cannon", to engineer a distributed-denial-of-service (DDoS) attack on two GitHub pages run by GreatFire.org, an advocacy organization dedicated to documenting and circumventing Internet censorship in China and cn-nytimes, a Chinese language version of The New York Times, launching the largest DDoS attack in the site's history as of 2015 (Marczak et al., 2015). However, despite the often adversarial relationship between GitHub and the Chinese government, China-based developers use the site because, unlike many platforms such as Facebook, Twitter, or Google, there is no commonly-used Chinese alternative to GitHub (Claburn, 2013).

While the technology industry in China is huge, service operators face unique challenges due to the country's strict regulatory environment. Any service provider operating in the Chinese market is required to comply with government content regulations. Commercial companies are held responsible for content on their platforms and are expected to dedicate resources to ensure compliance with relevant laws and regulations. Failure to do so can lead to fines or revocation of business licenses (MacKinnon, 2009).

This system is a form of intermediary liability or "self-discipline", which allows the government to shift responsibility for information control to the private sector (MacKinnon, 2010). While the response of commercial companies to regulations in China is well researched, the response of individuals providing Internet services is understudied, despite individuals also falling under many of these regulations (Ministry of Industry and Information Technology, 2005; OpenNet Initiative, 2006).

Laws and regulations on content control in China on content are broadly defined. In 2010, the State Council Information Office published a list of prohibited topics that are vaguely defined, such as "spreading rumors, disrupting social order and stability" and "transgressing social morality" (State Council Information Office and Ministry of Information Industry, 2005).

In 2017, the Cyberspace Administration of China (CAC), China's top-level Internet governance body, released four major regulations on Internet management, ranging from strengthening real-name registration requirements on Internet forums and online comments, to making individuals who host public accounts and moderate chat groups liable for content on the platforms (Cyberspace Administration of China, 2017a; Cyberspace Administration of China, 2017b; Cyberspace Administration of China, 2017c; Cyberspace Administration of China, 2017d). These regulations further push down the responsibility of content control down to individuals, a change which David Bandurski describes as "atomization and personalization of censorship" in China (Bandurski, 2017).

3 Methodology

In this section we describe (1) how we collect files, (2) how we extract lists of strings from these files, and (3) how we determine which of these lists are lists of sensitive blacklisted Chinese keywords.

3.1 Collecting files from GitHub

To collect files potentially containing Chinese keyword blacklists, we searched the popular code repository GitHub for keyword blacklists contained in files on the site. The files we searched were largely part of open source projects, but our search included any file publicly uploaded onto the site.

To search the site, we scraped the GitHub search function on their website. This step was necessary as, although GitHub has an API, it does not include full text search of all files across their entire site. Scraping websites can have ethical implications. In this case, scraping GitHub's web search was not allowed by their `robots.txt` file. Moreover, we did not want to deny service to any GitHub users by repeatedly making expensive search queries. To account for these concerns, we contacted GitHub's support team and communicated to them our desire to scrape their web search functionality. They permitted us to scrape their site, asking for the IP addresses of our measurement machines and the HTTP user agent string identifying our scraper. Moreover, they requested that our scraper not exceed ten HTTP requests per minute, as performing full site code search was computationally expensive. We wrote a scraper to automatically perform web searches, following up to the tenth page of results, returning at most 100 results, and complying with GitHub support's suggested rate limit.

To design our search queries, we first compiled a list of sensitive search words from publicly available Chinese blacklists reverse engineered from chat ("knowhow", 2004; Knockel et al., 2011; Crandall et al., 2013; Hardy, 2013) and live streaming (Knockel et al., 2015) apps. The former included QQ Games, TOM-Skype, Sina UC, and LINE. The latter included YY, 9158, Sina Show, and GuaGua. Together, we had over 21,934 unique keywords. As many of these keywords may be commonly mentioned in files not containing a sensitive keyword blacklist, we did not want to search for each of these keywords individually. Instead, we combined each sensitive keyword with each of the following blacklist-related strings to be found in either the file's name or contents: "badword", "banned", "blacklist", "censor", "dirty", "filter", "forbid", "forbidden", "illegal", "keyword", "profanity", or "sensitive". These strings were largely inspired by the names of files in previous work and by words we *a priori* speculated might be used.

As an optimization to reduce the number of HTTP requests necessary for each search, we first searched for each sensitive keyword by itself before combining it with each blacklist-related string. If the number of pages of results is no more than twelve, the number of blacklist-related strings we would combine it with, then we download all of the pages and manually filter out results that do not include blacklist-related strings in the files or file names. This step reduces the number of requests for such sensitive keywords as we do not have to make a separate request for each blacklist-related string. This strategy is especially more efficient for sensitive keywords that have no results or only one page of results, as only one request is necessary for such keywords as opposed to twelve.

We started scraping June 26 2016 and finished July 26 2016 after completing all search queries. For each of our search results, we downloaded each file corresponding to a search result in a separate stage of our process. We then converted each file to UTF-8 by using the `chardet` python package to detect each file's encoding, decoding it, and then re-encoding to UTF-8. Since we found that `chardet` often misclassified files as GB2312 or GBK containing GB18030 characters, we decoded all files classified as GB2312 and GBK as GB18030. If a file was encoded with a single byte encoding such as ASCII or Latin-1, we discarded the file as such an encoding does not have the ability to encode Chinese characters.

3.2 Extracting lists of strings from files

After downloading all files potentially containing Chinese blacklists and reencoding them to UTF-8, we extracted lists of strings from each file using a script we wrote called the *list extractor*. We used a heuristics approach to support a large variety of file formats. Our heuristics were based on (1) *a priori* assumptions about what file formats would be commonly used to store blacklisted keywords, (2) insights from previous work that reverse engineered keywords from applications (Crandall et al., 2013; Knockel et al., 2015; Knockel et al., 2017), and (3) different file formats that we found used to store blacklisted keywords in the files we downloaded from GitHub containing the word "法轮" (Falun), as Falun Gong is a taboo Chinese religious group referenced in all Chinese blacklists discovered in previous work (Crandall et al., 2013; Knockel et al., 2015; Knockel et al., 2017)

As a design goal we sought to keep the list extractor as simple as possible, and we were conscious to avoid overfitting to cases that seemed small or non-representative. Our list extractor was ultimately implemented in 348 lines of python3 source code, including comments and using typical whitespace conventions. It ultimately supported the following *formats* of files: XML, JSON, CSV, delimited plain text, C-like code, and newline-delimited plaintext. Our string extractor attempts to extract lists of strings from each file according to the formats listed in the above order. As a rule, we require that all lists have at least 20 strings and that they contain at least one Chinese character. If such a list is found using a format, then no other formats are attempted. In the remainder of this section, we outline our implementation of each format.

We first attempt to interpret each file as XML and parse it into a tree using a standard parser provided by python. If the file successfully parses, we then *flatten* the resulting tree by turning it into a list of pairs (x, y) where, for each attribute value or text node x, its path y consists of the names of all parent elements of x from the root node downward and, in the case of an attribute value, the name of the attribute key. We then consider all strings x with the same path y to be strings in the same list.

For XML, we also found that lists would often be contained within the text of a single XML attribute value or text node separated by a delimiter. Thus, we test each attribute value and text node to see if it contains a *delimited list*. A delimited list is a string containing delimiters, where a delimiter is one of the characters "`, |~;_@`", delimiting substrings that are no longer than 100 characters. Also, it must satisfy the requirements of any of our lists, namely that it contains at least 20 strings and that at least one of them contains a Chinese character.

Next, we attempt to parse the file as JSON using python's JSON parser. If the file successfully parses, we perform a flattening procedure to extract lists of strings similar to the one we do for XML, except building paths out of recursive JSON arrays and lists. Similar to XML, we check each string in the JSON to see if it contains a delimited list. Finally, as JSON inherently supports list-like data structures, we treat any JSON list where all elements are strings as a list of strings. Similarly, if any JSON array's keys are all strings or its values are all strings, then we treat those keys or values, respectively, as a list of strings.

After JSON, we attempt to parse the file as a CSV file, although we generally do not require that commas act as the separators. Although python includes support for parsing CSV files, we found the parser inadequate for our purposes, as it assumes that the input is a CSV file and is therefore quite liberal in what input it accepts. Contrary to this, we did not know if the file we were parsing was a CSV file, and so we wanted the parsing to consistently fail if the file was not a CSV.

To parse a CSV file, for each possible separator "`;,|^\t `" and for each possible quote symbol "`"'~`", we attempt to parse a first row of the CSV according to these separators and quote symbols and determine how many columns exist in the first row. If there are between two and ten columns, inclusive, we then attempt to parse the remainder of the file, according to the same separators and quote symbols and using the same number of columns as in the first row. If the parser finds that any row has a different number of columns, then the parsing of the file with that separator and quote symbol fails, and we then try any remaining unattempted combinations of separators and quote symbols. Lines containing only whitespace are ignored. If a file successfully parses as a CSV file, then, if it contains at least 20 rows, each column containing a Chinese character is considered a list.

Next, we attempt to parse the entire file itself as a plain delimited list, containing no other structured data.

After this, we attempt to treat the file as a C-like language. First, we remove all C- and C++-style comments from the file. Then we attempt to search it for arrays (`{...,...}`), lists (`[...,...]`), and tuples (`(...,...)`) of string literals (`"...\"..."` or `'...\'...'`), as well as delimited lists inside single string literals and regular expression literals such as those in Javascript (`/...\/.../`).

Finally, we attempt to treat the file as a plain newline-delimited list of strings. To distinguish such a file from any file containing multiple lines, we place some constraints on what files we accept based on what a Chinese blacklist would likely look like. First, if any line is not entirely whitespace and begins with at least three spaces, we reject the file, as indentation is a strong indication that the file contains structured data. Second, if the average length of all lines exceeds 15 characters, then we reject the file. Otherwise, if the file meets the usual list conditions, namely being at least 20 lines and containing a Chinese character, we accept it as a list of strings.

Another desirable format to have implemented would have been SQL. However, we found extracting lists from SQL problematic. The grammar of the language itself is not consistent between databases, and SQL allows diverse ways to insert list-like data into a database. With effort, we suspect that SQL could have been supported, but such an implementation would have been at odds with the design goals of keeping the string extractor simple and not overfitting to specific examples of data.

3.3 Determining whether lists of strings are Chinese blacklists

After we have extracted any potential lists of strings from each file, our final step is to classify each list as a *Chinese blacklist* or not. Our goal at this stage is to remove any non-blacklist-related lists of strings such as a list of Chinese cities including any list of strings extraneously extracted by our string extractor.

For purposes of this work, we consider a Chinese blacklist to be a list of sensitive keywords suitable for triggering censorship or surveillance that is primarily targeted at a Chinese audience. As a counterexample, we found that some projects in GitHub maintain lists of profane words from a large number of languages, including Chinese. In this work, we were not interested in detecting these lists, as they were not specifically targeting Chinese users and generally not made to comply with Chinese law.

To classify lists, we evaluate two approaches, (1) a *naive approach* based on searching for a single substring and (2) a more sophisticated *machine learning approach*. The naive approach works by positively classifying all lists that have any string containing "法轮" (Falun), referring to Falun Gong. We then manually validate each positively classified list to verify that it is indeed a Chinese blacklist. To extend the results, for each list containing "法轮", we additionally manually inspect that list's file for any other lists that may be Chinese blacklists and add any to the Chinese blacklists we had already found and verified. While this approach is simple, the weakness of it, however, is that it can only identify Chinese blacklists that either contain "法轮" or are in a file with a list containing "法轮".

To overcome this limitation, we also used a machine learning approach. We used a one-class support vector machine (SVM) (Schölkopf et al., 2001), as implemented by Scikit-learn (Pedregosa et al., 2011) and LIBSVM (Chang and Lin, 2011). We chose this machine learning classifier because it had the desired

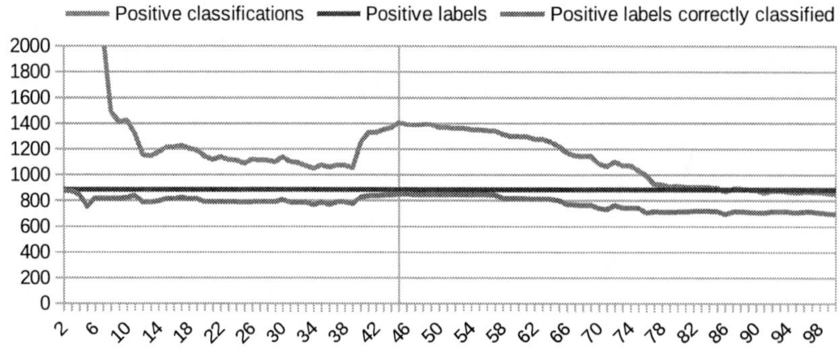

Figure 1: Classification performance for different d, the number of dimensions.

property of requiring training using only one class, the positive class, while still being able to classify something as either being in that class or not. This type of classifier was desirable because, although we had previous examples of Chinese blacklists to use to train a classifier, we had no representative sampling of all lists of strings on GitHub that are not Chinese blacklists.

The size of our training set was limited by the number of lists publicly available at the time of our work. Our training data consisted of the publicly available Chinese blacklists we used to design our search queries. We additionally used a list discovered in Google's Javascript code used to filter their mainland Chinese search engine ("caiguanhao", 2012). Overall, our training set consisted of 27 different Chinese blacklists.

In our model, we consider each list to be a vector of counts of the number of occurrences of each *Chinese word* in that list. We consider a Chinese word to be every consecutive string of Chinese characters in any of the strings in that list. For example, "历史de伤口" (history of wounds) contains two Chinese words, "历史" (history) and "伤口" (wound), separated by "de". As a preprocessing step, we also convert all traditional Chinese characters to simplified characters.

To reduce the dimensionality of this dataset, we use singular-value decomposition. Since we had all unlabeled data available at the time of training, we reduced dimensions over both the training data and the unlabeled data as a whole. Thus, in addition to making the classification computationally tractable, this allowed us to incorporate our unlabeled data into our training insofar as it is used to determine the final dimensions.

Since it was not obvious what number of dimensions to reduce our dataset to, we tried each number of dimensions d from 2 to 100. Cross-validating a one-class classifier is not generally feasible as there is no negative-labeled data to use for cross-validation. As a further difficulty, our training set was comparatively small compared to the number of lists that we could potentially detect.

To evaluate the best value of d, we used the verified Chinese blacklists discovered using our naive approach as positive labels for purposes of evaluating each d. We generally used the value of d that maximized the number of correctly classified positive labels. As with our naive approach, with the machine-learning approach we also manually verified each positive classification. Thus, we were not concerned with small increases to the false positive rate by maximizing the number of positively classified blacklists as long as it did not prohibitively burden our task of manually verifying positives by creating too many false positives.

4 Results

By scraping GitHub, we downloaded a total of 648,323 files. From these, using our list extractor, we extracted 45,986 lists containing at least 20 strings and at least one Chinese character.

Using our naive classification technique, we selected those lists with a string containing "法轮", yielding 915 potential Chinese blacklists. After manually verifying each list, we reduced this number to 838 true Chinese blacklists. By manually inspecting the other lists in the files containing these Chinese blacklists, we found an additional 46 Chinese blacklists, yielding a total of 884. Accounting for duplicates, we

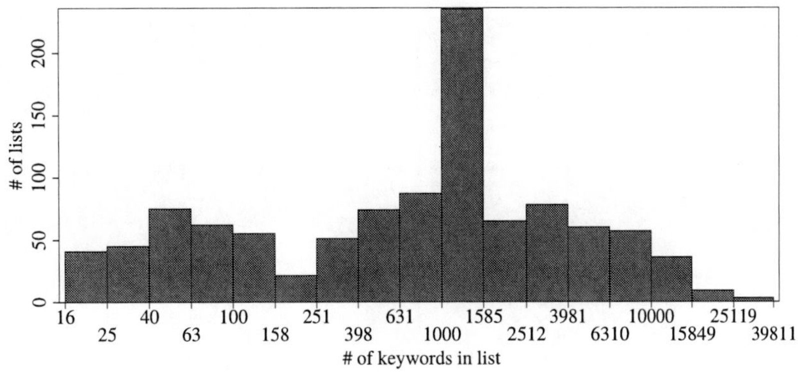

Figure 2: The distribution of the number of keywords in each list.

Top 1–10			Top 11–20		
n	Keyword	Translation	n	Keyword	Translation
703	鸡巴	dick	621	台独	Taiwanese independence
689	法轮	Falun	620	阴唇	labia
665	李洪志	Li Hongzhi	618	真善忍	truthfulness, tolerance
640	阴道	vagina	616	疆独	Xinjiang independence
638	阴茎	penis	616	做爱	making love
635	藏独	Tibetan independence	611	口交	blowjob
633	龟头	glans	604	法轮功	Falun Gong
629	淫水	kinky	597	性交	sex
626	肛交	anal sex	596	共匪	CCP bandit
622	小穴	small hole	593	江泽民	Jiang Zemin

Table 1: Top 20 keywords as ranked by n, the number of lists each keyword appears in.

overall found 451 unique Chinese blacklists using this technique.

Using our machine learning technique, in Figure 1, for each number of dimensions d, we show the number of positive classifications and the number of positive labels correctly classified. For $d > 3$, the maximum number of positive labels correctly classified, 852, occurs at $d = 46$. For degenerate values of d, $d = 2$ and $d = 3$, more of the positive labels were positively classified; however, for both of these d, the number of positively classified lists is over 20,000, which is nearly half of our unlabeled dataset.

Using $d = 46$, our machine learning approach positively classified 1,391 lists. After manually verifying them, we found that 1,054 of the positive classifications were true Chinese blacklists. Accounting for duplicates, there were 524 unique Chinese blacklists. Together these lists comprised 215,007 unique keywords. In the remainder of this section, we characterize these 1,054 true Chinese blacklists that we collected using the machine learning approach.

The Chinese blacklists we discovered contained a varying number of keywords. Since our methodology only considered lists with at least 20 keywords, all lists that we found had at least that many. The longest blacklist we found contains 38,237 keywords. The mean length was approximately 2,128 keywords, and the median length was 1,026 keywords. See Figure 2 for a plot of the distribution.

The blacklists contained a variety of different sensitive keywords. Table 1 shows the top 20 keywords most commonly occurring on the lists. These keywords reflected prurient interests (鸡巴, "dick"), Falun Gong references (法轮, "Falun"; 李洪志, "Li Hongzhi", the founder of Falun Gong), political movements (藏独, "Tibetan independence"), government criticism (共匪, "CCP bandit"), and political leaders (江泽民, "Jiang Zemin").

Despite a small number of words being on most lists, we found that blacklists were typically very dis-

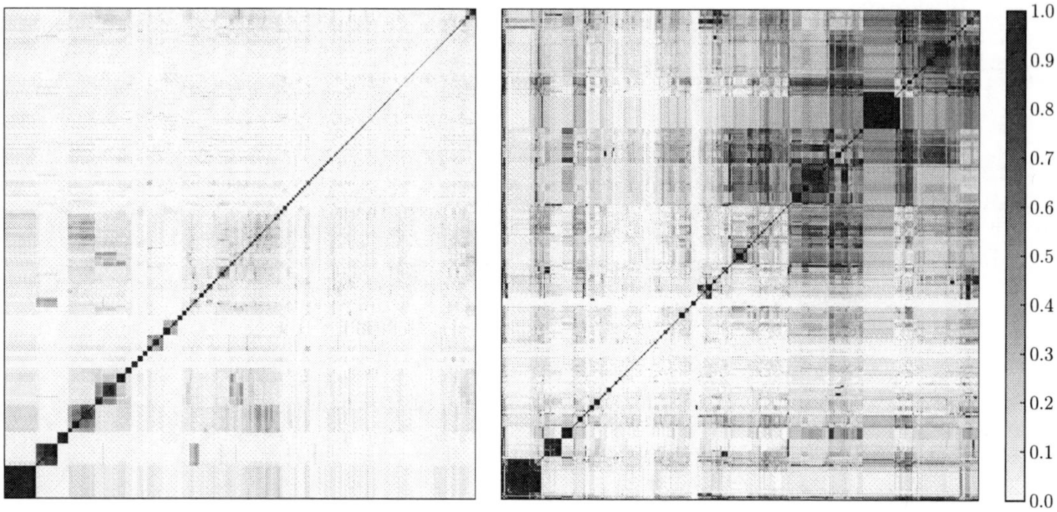

Figure 3: Left, lists clustered by Jaccard similarity; right, lists clustered by $\textit{similarity}(x, y) = \max(\%\text{ of } x \text{ in } y, \%\text{ of } y \text{ in } x)$.

similar. We compared the inter-similarity between blacklists using two metrics. The first metric compares their Jaccard similarity, which is the size of the set intersection of both lists divided by their set union. The second metric, for two lists x and y, computes $\max(\%\text{ of } x \text{ in } y, \%\text{ of } y \text{ in } x)$. This metric is designed to tease out relationships where one list was built using another; however, using this metric, small lists which typically contain mostly commonly blacklisted words tend to be very similar to large lists that tend to inevitably contain them as well. Figure 3 shows the lists compared using each metric and clustered according to the centroid linkage method (Müllner, 2011).

The heat maps reveal very little overlap between lists. This finding is consistent with studies analyzing the implementation of censorship on Chinese chat clients, live streaming apps, and mobile games (Crandall et al., 2013; Knockel et al., 2015; Knockel et al., 2017) by commercial companies. These studies found that, rather than Chinese censorship being top-down and monolithic, it is a decentralized system where developers are liable for deciding what to censor themselves. The unprecedented quantity of lists in our study raises new questions regarding how so many disparate lists are being created, especially since they are so large, with over half of them having over one thousand keywords.

5 Conclusion and future work

In this work we scraped GitHub for files containing sensitive Chinese keywords and strings related to blacklists. From these files, we used a novel heuristics-based tool to extract lists of strings from a number of structured data formats. We then used a machine learning technique to determine which of these lists represent Chinese blacklists. Overall, we found over 1,000 Chinese blacklists comprising over 200,000 unique keywords, representing the largest dataset of Chinese keyword blacklists collected to date. These results provide multiple avenues for future research particularly around what motivates individual developers to include these lists in their projects and how the lists are created.

It remains an open question why developers include these lists in their projects. The developers may be concerned that they themselves or others using or deploying their projects may be held liable for content shared on their projects in the same manner that commercial companies are known to be controlled. Developers may be accustomed to this requirement and see it as necessary for their project to gain users and traction in the Chinese market. It may also be that they believe their application should be censored and share the political concerns that motivate the Chinese government.

Most of the lists we discovered had over 1,000 keywords, which seems too large for a developer to individually compile, yet given the dissimilarity between lists, they do not appear to come from common sources either. GitHub projects include contact information making it possible to consider an interview of the developers to gain insight into their motivations and process for creating the lists. We found little similarity between lists in terms of specific keywords, suggesting that these lists were independently curated. Categorization of the keywords according to high level topic would allow testing whether lists have similarity when comparing their high level topic coverage.

Another avenue of future work is to further utilize data in GitHub to understand Chinese censorship. In this work we sampled projects containing Chinese blacklists; however, another research direction is to sample all China-based projects independently of if they perform censorship. This approach would allow us to characterize what types and what proportion of China-based projects on GitHub perform filtering versus those which do not. GitHub also contains valuable metadata unexplored by this work. Analyzing blacklists' git commit history may allow researchers to if and how blacklists are updated over time. Moreover, GitHub social networking data tracking forks, stars, and watchers may provide insight into if and how lists are shared over the platform.

Acknowledgments

This research was supported by the Open Society Foundations. Jeffrey Knockel's research for this project was supported by the Open Technology Fund's Information Control Fellowship Program.

Keyword list data is available at `https://github.com/citizenlab/chat-censorship/tree/master/open-source`.

References

Bai Tiantian. 2013. China's GitHub Censorship Dilemma. Available at http://www.globaltimes.cn/content/757868.shtml.

David Bamman, Brendan O'Connor, and Noah A. Smith. 2012. Censorship and deletion practices in Chinese social media. *First Monday*, 17(3).

David Bandurski. 2017. The Great Hive of Propaganda. Available at http://chinamediaproject.org/2017/09/16/the-great-hive-of-propaganda/.

"caiguanhao". 2012. Google收集的GFW屏蔽关键词（敏感词）. Available at https://caiguanhao.wordpress.com/2012/06/01/google-gfw-blacklist/.

Chih-Chung Chang and Chih-Jen Lin. 2011. LIBSVM: A library for support vector machines. *ACM Transactions on Intelligent Systems and Technology*, 2:27:1–27:27. Software available at http://www.csie.ntu.edu.tw/~cjlin/libsvm.

Thomas Claburn. 2013. China's GitHub Censorship Dilemma. Available at https://www.informationweek.com/software/social/chinas-GitHub-censorship-dilemma/d/d-id/1108436.

Jedidiah R. Crandall, Masashi Crete-Nishihata, Jeffrey Knockel, Sarah McKune, Adam Senft, Diana Tseng, and Greg Wiseman. 2013. Chat program censorship and surveillance in China: Tracking TOM-Skype and Sina UC. *First Monday*, 18(7), 6.

Masashi Crete-Nishihata, Andrew Hilts, Jeffrey Knockel, Jason Q. Ng, Lotus Ruan, and Greg Wiseman. 2016. Harmonized Histories? A year of fragmented censorship across Chinese live streaming applications. Technical report, Citizen Lab, University of Toronto. Available at https://netalert.me/assets/harmonized-histories/harmonized-histories.pdf.

Cyberspace Administration of China. 2017a. 互联网用户公众账号信息服务管理规定. Available at http://www.cac.gov.cn/2017-09/07/c_1121624269.htm.

Cyberspace Administration of China. 2017b. 互联网群组信息服务管理规定. Available at http://www.cac.gov.cn/2017-09/07/c_1121623889.htm.

Cyberspace Administration of China. 2017c. 互联网论坛社区服务管理规定. Available at http://www.cac.gov.cn/2017-08/25/c_1121541921.htm.

Cyberspace Administration of China. 2017d. 互联网跟帖评论服务管理规定. Available at http://www.cac.gov.cn/2017-08/25/c_1121541842.htm.

GitHub. 2017. GitHub Octoverse 2017. Available at https://octoverse.github.com/.

GreatFire. 2013. China, GitHub and the man-in-the-middle. Available at https://en.greatfire.org/blog/2013/jan/china-github-and-man-middle.

Seth Hardy. 2013. Asia Chats: Investigating Regionally-based Keyword Censorship in LINE. Technical report, Citizen Lab, University of Toronto. Available at https://citizenlab.ca/2013/11/asia-chats-investigating-regionally-based-keyword-censorship-line/.

Jeffrey Knockel, Jedidiah R. Crandall, and Jared Saia. 2011. Three researchers, five conjectures: An empirical analysis of TOM-Skype censorship and surveillance. In *FOCI'11 (USENIX Workshop on Free and Open Communications on the Internet)*.

Jeffrey Knockel, Masashi Crete-Nishihata, Jason Q. Ng, Adam Senft, and Jedidiah R. Crandall. 2015. Every Rose Has Its Thorn: Censorship and Surveillance on Social Video Platforms in China. In *5th USENIX Workshop on Free and Open Communications on the Internet (FOCI 15)*.

Jeffrey Knockel, Lotus Ruan, and Masashi Crete-Nishihata. 2017. Measuring Decentralization of Chinese Keyword Censorship via Mobile Games. In *7th USENIX Workshop on Free and Open Communications on the Internet (FOCI 17)*.

"knowhow". 2004. QQ过滤词列表 zt. Available at https://web.archive.org/web/20040908030852/http://bbs.omnitalk.org/arts/messages/3824.html.

Rebecca MacKinnon. 2009. China's Censorship 2.0: How companies censor bloggers. *First Monday; Volume 14, Number 2 - 2 February 2009*.

Rebecca MacKinnon. 2010. Google's China troubles continue; Congress examines U.S. investment in Chinese censorship. Available at http://rconversation.blogs.com/rconversation/2010/06/index.html.

Rebecca MacKinnon. 2011. China's "Networked Authoritarianism". *Journal of Democracy*, 22(2):32–46.

Bill Marczak, Nicholas Weaver, Jakub Dalek, Roya Ensafi, David Fifield, Sarah McKune, Arn Rey, John Scott-Railton, Ronald Deibert, and Vern Paxson. 2015. China's Great Cannon. Technical report, Citizen Lab, University of Toronto. Available at https://citizenlab.org/2015/04/chinas-great-cannon/.

Blake Miller. 2017. The Limits of Commercialized Censorship in China. Available at http://www.blakeapm.com/research/censorship.

Ministry of Industry and Information Technology. 2005. 非经营性互联网信息服务备案管理办法. Available at http://www.miit.gov.cn/n1146295/n1146557/n1146624/c3554618/content.html.

Daniel Müllner. 2011. Modern hierarchical, agglomerative clustering algorithms. *arXiv preprint arXiv:1109.2378*.

Open Source China. 2016. GitHub 中国区前 100 名到底是什么样的人? . Available at https://www.oschina.net/news/72235/github-china-100.

OpenNet Initiative. 2006. 非经营性互联网信息服务备案管理办法. Available at https://opennet.net/bulletins/011/.

F. Pedregosa, G. Varoquaux, A. Gramfort, V. Michel, B. Thirion, O. Grisel, M. Blondel, P. Prettenhofer, R. Weiss, V. Dubourg, J. Vanderplas, A. Passos, D. Cournapeau, M. Brucher, M. Perrot, and E. Duchesnay. 2011. Scikit-learn: Machine learning in Python. *Journal of Machine Learning Research*, 12:2825–2830.

Emil Protalinski. 2013. The Chinese government appears to be blocking GitHub via DNS (Update: Investigation underway). Available at https://thenextweb.com/asia/2013/01/21/the-chinese-government-appears-to-have-completely-blocked-github-via-dns/.

Lotus Ruan, Jeffrey Knockel, Jason Q. Ng, and Masashi Crete-Nishihata. 2016. One App, Two Systems: How WeChat uses one censorship policy in China and another internationally. Technical report, Citizen Lab, University of Toronto. Available at https://citizenlab.ca/2016/11/wechat-china-censorship-one-app-two-systems/.

Bernhard Schölkopf, John C. Platt, John Shawe-Taylor, Alex J. Smola, and Robert C. Williamson. 2001. Estimating the support of a high-dimensional distribution. *Neural computation*, 13(7):1443–1471.

State Council Information Office and Ministry of Information Industry. 2005. Provisions on the Administration of Internet News Information Services. Available at `http://www.cecc.gov/pages/virtualAcad/index.phpd?showsingle=24396`.

Nart Villeneuve. 2006. The filtering matrix: integrated mechanisms of information control and the demarcation of borders in cyberspace. *First Monday*, 11(1).

崔绮雯. 2015. 已经被攻击了一百多小时的GitHub为什么那么重要? . Available at `https://www.qdaily.com/articles/7938.html`.

雅楠. 2013. 12306抢票插件拖垮美国代码托管站Github. Available at `http://tech.sina.com.cn/i/csj/2013-01-16/19367984516.shtml`.

Linguistic Characteristics of Censorable Language on SinaWeibo

Kei Yin Ng   Anna Feldman   Jing Peng   Chris Leberknight
Montclair State University
Montclair, New Jersey, USA
{ngk2,feldmana,pengj,leberknightc}@montclair.edu

Abstract

This paper investigates censorship from a linguistic perspective. We collect a corpus of censored and uncensored posts on a number of topics, build a classifier that predicts censorship decisions independent of discussion topics. Our investigation reveals that the strongest linguistic indicator of censored content of our corpus is its readability.

1 Introduction

More than half of the world's Internet users are still restricted to a censored World Wide Web[1] and do not have access to a lot of public information on the Internet. This work is concerned with censorship directed at voices critical of the ruling government, which is common in authoritarian and repressive regimes. Our study takes a closer look at the censorship activities in mainland China, with a particular focus on one of its mainstream social media platforms – Sina Weibo. Internet censorship in mainland China consists of several layers: restricted access to certain websites, restricted access to certain keyword search results, and removal of certain information published by Internet users. Since censorship on social media typically happens after a user has successfully published on the platform, what gets censored or not is largely a "real-time" decision due to the unpredictable nature of published content. Discussions on sensitive topics do not always get censored, as evidenced by their accessibility on the platform. So what determines a sensitive discussion to stay or to be censored? This study investigates the factors that contribute to censorship on Sina Weibo from a linguistic perspective. We locate sources that provide censored and uncensored Weibo texts, extract linguistic features from the corpus we collect and build a classifier that predicts censorship decisions independent of discussion topics. We think that identifying linguistic properties of censored content, regardless of topic, will help develop techniques to circumvent censorship.

2 Related Work

Many measurement and circumvention studies focus more on exploiting technological limitations with existing routing protocols (Leberknight et al., 2012; Katti et al., 2005; Levin et al., 2015; McPherson et al., 2016; Weinberg et al., 2012)). However, little attention has focused on *linguistically*-inspired techniques to study online censorship. One notable exception applies linguistic steganography to obfuscate censored content (Safaka et al., 2016). Their results focus purely on circumvention while this research takes a linguistic approach to detect censorable content. In recent years, several detection mechanisms have been proposed to observe and categorize the type of content and keywords that are censored (Knockel et al., 2015; Zhu et al., 2013). King et al. (2013) analyze the content of censored and uncensored texts from various Chinese social media sources to study the relationship between criticism of the state and chance of censorship. Their main findings suggest that negative comments about the state do not always lead to censorship. Rather, the presence of Collective Action Potential (the potential to cause collective action in real life) is what makes a post susceptible to censorship. Lee (2016) explores the effectiveness of linguistic tactics in circumventing online censorship in China and argued that using

[1] freedomhouse.org

Proceedings of the First Workshop on Natural Language Processing for Internet Freedom, pages 12–22
Santa Fe, New Mexico, USA, August 20, 2018.

parodic satire could most likely survive censorship due to the nature of parodic satire – indirect and relies heavily on users' and censors' ability to interpret based on context. Hiruncharoenvate et al. (2015) discover linguistically-informed ways to delay the detection and removal of content on Chinese social media. Their findings show that the use of homophones of censored keywords on Sina Weibo could help extend the time a Weibo post could remain available online. However, the methods of King et al. (2013), Lee (2016) and Hiruncharoenvate et al. (2015) all rely on a significant amount of human effort to interpret and annotate texts to evaluate the likeliness of censorship, which might not be practical to carry out for common Internet users in real life. Bamman et al. (2012) uncover a set of politically sensitive keywords and find that the presence of some of them in a Weibo blogpost contribute to higher chance of the post being censored. Our approach is not quite the same as Bamman et al. We target a set of topics that have been suggested to be sensitive and cover areas not limited to politics. We then study the linguistic components of both the censored and uncensored posts on those topics. In this way, we are looking beyond the mere existence of sensitive keywords in contributing to censorship. We are trying to investigate how the textual content as a whole might be relevant to censorship decision when both the censored and uncensored blogposts include the same sensitive keyword(s).

3 Hypotheses

Our experiments are based on a number of ideas from the field of psychology.

1. Uncensored content is easier for readers to process than censored content Research in psychology (e.g., Lewandowsky et al.(2012)) claims that rejecting information requires cognitive effort whereas accepting information as truth is easier because detecting false information requires additional motivational and cognitive resources. Another point of view in psychology (e.g. Schwartz et al. (2008)) suggests that people tend to make judgments based on their subjective feelings of how easy it is to recall or process information. According to this group of psychologists, people do not have pre-existing, stable attitudes on many issues. Instead, their opinions are constructed on the spot and contexts (mood, emotion, ease of processing, etc.) determines the influence of the material they read and see. Since censorship manipulates information availability, we consider it an agent that creates misinformed online experiences. By eliminating certain content, the censors are trying to present events and opinions in a biased way. Based on the claims made by the research mentioned above, we hypothesize that uncensored content is easier for readers to process (or maybe even to believe) than censored content. The features described in the following sections try to address this assumption by showing that texts that have high readability scores (i.e., easy to process) tend to be left uncensored. We explore the psychological meaning of words and develop new readability metrics to test this hypothesis.

2. Censored and uncensored texts should have their own unique linguistic characteristics. Sali et al. (2016) claim that we all have tendency to choose information that we are more frequently exposed to. We hypothesize that censored and uncensored blogposts, regardless of topics, will have their own unique recurrent themes and characteristics.

4 Data collection

We collect a corpus of censored and uncensored texts in order to analyze and compare the linguistic signals embedded in each category[2].

4.1 The Corpus

Our corpus contains censored and uncensored microblogposts on scandalous issues happened or happening in mainland China. The selection of these issues is inspired by a set of lexicon, namely the Grass-mud Horse Lexicon, devised and widely used by Chinese Internet users as a political satire. Past studies have shown the relevance and significance of this lexicon in facilitating online political and social discussion among Chinese Internet users (Wang (2012), Tang and Yang (2011)). Therefore, the lexicon can be regarded as an indicator of scandalous issues in the mainland Chinese society. Most issues covered in our

[2]https://github.com/bondfeld/Datasets

Issue	Date	Search Term(s)	Censored Quantity	Uncensored Quantity
air pollution	3/2013 - 12/2017	smog (雾霾)	223	240
gutter oil	4/2012 - 9/2017	gutter oil (地沟油)	120	138
milk scandal	4/2012 - 7/2017	melamine (三聚氰胺) & toxic formula (毒奶粉)	49	85
Internet censorship	9/2013 - 11/2017	censor (屏蔽)	195	216
Internet propaganda	7/2014 - 12/2017	fifty-cent (五毛)	258	290
Bo Xilai	1/2015 - 11/2017	Bo Xilai (薄熙来)	125	75
kindergarten abuse	11/2017 - 12/2017	RYB (红黄蓝)	53	94

Table 1: Published date range, search term(s) used, and quantity of each issue

data are described in the lexicon and the relevant blogposts are retrievable using relevant search terms. Table 1 shows the quantity and published date range of blogposts of each issue, and also the search keyword used to obtain the blogposts. The issues are divided into four categories as below.

4.1.1 Pollution and Food Safety

This category consists of blogposts relevant to three scandalous incidents. The first is about the use of *Gutter Oil* in mainland China. It was reported in 2010 that a significant number of restaurants used gutter oil as cooking oil. Long-term consumption of gutter oil is believed to cause stomach and liver cancer. The second issue is the *Milk Scandal* in 2008 when milk and infant formula made in mainland China were found to be adulterated with melamine to make the products appeared to have high protein content. This caused over 50,000 infants to be hospitalized. The third issue is the ongoing severe *Air Pollution* problem in some cities in mainland China.

4.1.2 Internet Censorship and Propaganda

This category consists of blogposts that discuss two issues - the Internet censorship and the Internet propaganda activities on Chinese social media platforms and websites. For the propaganda issue, we target blogposts that talk about the "fifty-cent party"(五毛党), a group of commentators that is believed to be hired by the Chinese authorities to manipulate public opinion in favor of the Chinese Communist Party.

4.1.3 Bo Xilai

This category is about *Bo Xilai*(薄熙来), a former Communist Party chief in Chongqing. In 2013, he was found guilty of corruption and was expelled from the Communist Party, parliament and sentenced to life imprisonment.

4.1.4 Kindergarten Abuse

This category is about a recent case of *Kindergarten Abuse* in Beijing. In November, 2017, toddlers at a nursery called RYB(红黄蓝) were reported to be molested, spiked with needles and drugged with mysterious white pills.

4.2 Sources

4.2.1 Uncensored Data

All uncensored blogposts are collected from Sina Weibo[3]. Sina Weibo is regarded as one of the most popular social media platforms in mainland China. It functions similarly as Twitter where users can publish, reblog and repost opinions and news on any topic. Although users can publish freely on Weibo, the published content is subject to scrutiny and would possibly be censored or deleted if it is considered to have violated Weibo's policies. Therefore, content that can be found on Sina Weibo has already passed the censorship mechanisms and is regarded as uncensored.

4.2.2 Censored Data

All censored data are collected from Freeweibo[4] and WeiboScope[5]. Both sources tracked censored blogposts from Sina Weibo and make them available to the public. Below are some examples of censored and uncensored posts with their English translations:

Censored - Bo Xilai: 薄熙来是今天的高岗，周永康是今天的康生，两位都是为党和国家立下汗马功劳的人，也都是被政治斗争构陷的人。
Bo Xilai is today's Gao Gang. Zhou Yongkang is today's Kang Sheng. They both made great contributions to the Party and the country. They both got framed by political infighting.
Censored - Kindergarten: 每次看到这样的新闻，我都宁愿这件事情的结局是有人造谣，然后我因为传播谣言被逮进去蹲几天也不希望是真的。到底能不能来个解释啊真是日狗了！ Every time I read this kind of news, I'd rather believe they're just made-up stories. I'd rather get arrested and sent to jail for a couple of days for spreading untrue rumors than knowing the stories are real. Can anyone just give an explanation? This is really frustrating!

Uncensored Bo Xilai: 薄熙来始终不认罪，戴械具，老周认罪，不戴，好看点。 Bo Xilai still isn't pleading guilty. And he's cuffed. Old Zhao pleaded guilty, and he's not cuffed. That looked better.
Uncensored Kindergarten: 从携程亲子园到红黄蓝幼儿园，"虐童"案再次成为焦点，只希望类似的事件从此不会发生，希望澄清的一切都是事实的真相，希望所有的小朋友都在阳光下健康成长。
From Ctrip Day Care to RYB Kindergarten, "child abuse" has once again become the news highlight. I just hope nothing similar will happen again, and all the clarifications are the truth. I hope all children can grow up healthily under the sun.

4.3 Data Selection and Preprocessing

To ensure that a bloggpost's original text content is the only factor that renders it being censored or uncensored, only blogposts that do not contain any images, hyperlinks or reblogged content are selected. Some blogposts returned by key-term search are not irrelevant to our target issues because of the multiple word senses or meanings of search terms. We filter out all irrelevant blogposts. Due to the fact that the availability of censored data from the sources described above are lower (except the Bo Xilai issue), we first collect all available censored blogposts, and then based on the quantity of censored blogposts we collect corresponding number of uncensored blogposts that were published in the same date range as the censored counterpart. Name of author, friend tags and hashtags are removed from all data. Finally, since the Chinese language does not have word boundaries, word segmentation has to be carried out before certain linguistic features can be extracted. We use Jieba[6] to segment all the data. The performance of Jeiba on our data has been manually checked to ensure quality. In cases of mis-segmentation, Jieba allows manual specification of mis-segmented words to improve accuracy.

5 Linguistic Features

We extract features described below for building classifiers.

Sensitive Keywords We collect keywords that are regarded as sensitive in mainland China and count the frequency of keywords in each blogpost. The first source is a list of blacklisted keywords provided by Wikipedia[7] and the second source is a list of sensitive Sina Weibo search terms provided by China

[3]https://www.weibo.com/

[4]https://freeweibo.com

[5]http://weiboscope.jmsc.hku.hk

[6]https://github.com/fxsjy/jieba

[7]https://en.wikipedia.org/wiki/List_of_blacklisted_keywords_in_China

Digital Times[8]. As accessibility of search results change from time to time, China Digital Times tests the "searchability" of each keyword and records the date of testing for reference. For each issue, we collect keywords that have been tested during the same time period as the published date of the blogposts.

Sentiment We use BaiduAI[9] to obtain a set of sentiment scores for each blogpost. While the sentiment analyzer of BaiduAI is not designed specifically for Weibo texts, it targets customer reviews and other "comment type" of texts. We find it suitable to apply on Weibo texts which share similar characteristics with those text types. The sentiment analyzer provides a positive sentiment percentage score and a negative sentiment percentage score for each post, which sum to 1.

LIWC The English Linguistic Inquiry and Word Count (LIWC) (Pennebaker et al., 2017; Pennebaker et al., 2015) is a program that analyzes text on a word-by-word basis, calculating percentage of words that match each language dimension. LIWC is built on dominant theories in psychology, business, and medicine and provides word categories representing the various types of words such as personal pronouns, verbs, tenses as well as many other linguistic and psychological categories. The Chinese LIWC dictionary is developed by Huang et al. (2012) based on the English LIWC dictionary. It is built by first translating from the English LIWC, and then further developed and modified to accommodate the linguistic differences between English and Chinese. We use the Chinese LIWC to extract the frequency of word categories. Altogether we extract 95 features from LIWC.

Word frequency (WordFreq) Inspired by Zheng (2005) on assessing readability of Chinese text, we calculate the average frequency of words in each Weibo post based on Aihanyu's CNCorpus of modern Chinese[10]. It is a corpus that consists of about 9.5 million Chinese words. Word frequency of the corpus provides a picture of how often a certain word is used in modern Chinese texts. The lower the frequency, the less commonly used a word is. For words that appear very rarely (less than 50 times in the corpus), we count their frequency as 0.0001%.

Character frequency (CharFreq) Besides word frequency, we also extract character frequency based on the character frequency list of modern Chinese compiled by Da (2004)[11]. The idea is similar to word frequency – the lower the character frequency, the less commonly used a character is.

Semantic classes Zheng (2005) discusses the insufficiency of relying on word frequency alone to assess text readability. The semantics of words should also be taken into consideration. The Chinese Thesaurus 同义词词林 (developed by Mei (1984) and extended by HIT-SCIR[12]) divides words into 12 semantic classes (Human, Matter, Space and time, Abstract matter, Characteristics, Actions, Psychology, Human activities, States and phenomena, Relations, Auxiliary words, and Formulaic expressions). A word might belong to more than one semantic class. For example, the word 上 belongs to 7 classes: Space and time, Abstract matter, Characteristics, Actions, Human activities, State and phenomena, and Relations. The more semantic classes a word belongs to, the more semantic variety it has. The idea is that more semantic variety requires more mental processing to interpret such word in relation to its surrounding context, and hence contributes to a higher difficulty level of the text. We count the number of distinct semantic classes found in each post, normalize by dividing the number of words by the number of semantic classes.

Readability 1 Inspired by Zheng (2005)'s discussion on the effectiveness of determining text readability with the number of distinct semantic classes a sentence has, and the insufficiency of using word frequency or word count alone to decide readability, we combine the use of frequency and semantic classes to form a readability metric for our data. We take the mean of character frequency, word frequency and word count to semantic groups ratio as a score of text readability. For each individual component, a lower score means a lower readability (more difficult to read and understand). Therefore, the lower the mean of the 3 components, the lower readability a text has. While our metric has not been formally tested, its components overlap with that of Sung et al. (2015) on the word level and semantic level. Their

[8]https://chinadigitaltimes.net/china/sensitive-words-series/

[9]https://ai.baidu.com

[10]http://www.aihanyu.org/cncorpus/index.aspx

[11]http://lingua.mtsu.edu/chinese-computing/statistics/

[12]Harbin Institute of Technology Research Center for Social Computing and Information Retrieval.

readability metric has been tested and validated to measure the readability of Chinese written texts for native speakers.

Idioms The part-of-speech tagger provided by Jieba annotates idioms. Most Chinese idioms are phrases that consist of 4 characters. The idiom outputs are manually checked to ensure tagging accuracy. In total, 399 and 259 idioms are extracted from censored and uncensored blogposts respectively. We normalize the raw count of idioms by the number of words in the blogpost. To see whether the presence of idioms would potentially affect the readability of a text, we calculate the correlation coefficient between the readability score (see Section 5) and the number of idioms divided by word count. We find a negative correlation between the two, suggesting that the higher the number of idioms in a text, the lower its readability.

Readability 2 To further investigate how idioms might interact with the readability feature, we incorporate the inverse of normalized idioms into our readability metrics to create a second version of the readability score. Both versions are used as features for classification. In cases where the normalized idiom is 0, we re-scale it to 0.01.

Word embeddings and eigenfeatures We use distributed word representations (word embeddings) as features. We train word vectors using the word2vec tool (Mikolov et al., 2013a; Mikolov et al., 2013b) on 300,000 of the latest Chinese articles[13] provided by Wikipedia. We then remove stop-words from each blogpost in our censorship corpus. For each word in the blog post, we compute a 200 dimensional vector. Since the number of words associated with each blogpost is different, we compute the 200x200 covariance matrix for each document and determine the eigen decomposition of this matrix. The eigenvectors are the directions in which the data varies the most. We use the eigenvalues as features to represent our data. The last 40 eigenvalues capture about 85% of total variance and are therefore used as features.

6 Censorship: The Human Baseline

We carried out a crowdsourcing experiment on Amazon Mechanical Turk[14] on the Bo Xilai data. We present all blogposts one by one and ask participants to decide whether they think a post has been censored (Yes) or has not been censored (No) on Sina Weibo. To make sure the results are reliable, four control questions are included to test participants' knowledge on the Chinese language and the Bo Xilai incident (Please see Appendix 1). Only responses that correctly answer all four control questions are accepted and analyzed. The same experiment is also presented as a survey to five acquaintances of the author who are native Chinese speakers and are knowledgeable of the Bo Xilai incident and Internet censorship in mainland China. In total, we collect responses from 23 participants. Not all 23 participants answered all posts. Each post has been judged by four to eight different participants. The average accuracy of the human judges is 63.51% which serves as our human baseline. The interannotator agreement, however, is low (Cohen's kappa (Cohen, 1960)) is 0.07), which suggests that the task of deciding what blogpost has been censored is extremely difficult.

7 Machine Learning Classification

Features		Censored			Uncensored		
	Acc	Pre	Rec	F1	Pre	Rec	F1
NB all (147)	0.65	0.76	0.65	0.70	0.53	0.65	0.58
NB eigenvalues (40)	0.57	0.69	0.57	0.62	0.43	0.57	0.50
NB ling. features (107)	0.64	0.76	0.61	0.68	0.51	0.68	0.58
NB best features(17)	0.67	0.74	0.74	0.74	0.56	0.56	0.56
SMO all (147)	0.70	0.75	0.78	0.77	0.61	0.56	0.58
SMO eigenvalues (40)	0.62	0.63	0.92	0.75	0.44	0.11	0.17
SMO ling. features (107)	0.68	0.74	0.74	0.74	0.57	0.57	0.57
SMO best features (17)	0.72	0.71	0.91	0.80	0.73	0.39	0.50
majority class	0.63						

Table 2: Classification results for the Bo Xilai subcorpus.

[13] https://dumps.wikimedia.org/zhwiki/latest/

[14] https://www.mturk.com

Features	Acc	Censored Pre	Censored Rec	Censored F1	Uncensored Pre	Uncensored Rec	Uncensored F1
NB all (147)	0.63	0.49	0.64	0.55	0.75	0.62	0.68
NB eigenvalues (40)	0.58	0.45	0.72	0.55	0.76	0.50	0.60
NB ling. features (107)	0.64	0.50	0.59	0.54	0.74	0.67	0.70
NB best features (9)	0.72	0.64	0.53	0.58	0.76	0.83	0.72
SMO all (147)	0.63	0.47	0.34	0.40	0.68	0.79	0.73
SMO eigenvalues (40)	0.63	0.00	0.00	0.00	0.64	0.99	0.78
SMO ling. features (107)	0.65	0.53	0.36	0.43	0.69	0.82	0.75
SMO best features (9)	0.70	0.91	0.19	0.31	0.68	0.99	0.81
majority class	0.64						

Table 3: Classification results for the Kindergarten Abuse subcorpus.

Features	Acc	Censored Pre	Censored Rec	Censored F1	Uncensored Pre	Uncensored Rec	Uncensored F1
NB all (147)	0.66	0.60	0.76	0.67	0.74	0.57	0.64
NB eigenvalues (40)	0.62	0.57	0.68	0.62	0.68	0.57	0.62
NB ling. features (107)	0.69	0.63	0.78	0.70	0.77	0.61	0.68
NB best features(69)	0.67	0.62	0.74	0.67	0.74	0.61	0.67
SMO all (147)	0.71	0.70	0.66	0.68	0.73	0.76	0.74
SMO eigenvalues (40)	0.60	0.56	0.63	0.59	0.65	0.58	0.61
SMO ling. features (107)	0.72	0.70	0.68	0.69	0.74	0.75	0.75
SMO best features (69)	0.71	0.69	0.68	0.68	0.73	0.74	0.73
majority class	0.54						

Table 4: Classification results for the Pollution & Food Safety subcorpus.

7.1 Naive Bayes and Support Vector Machine

We extract 107 linguistic features described above and 40 eigenvalues (as they capture around 85% of total variance, see section 5) for each blogpost. The 107 linguistic features for each blogpost are first standardized as a z-score (the standard score) before proceeding to classification. Then, for each of the 4 sub-corpora, we build a standard Naive Bayes (John and Langley, 1995) classifier and a linear Support Vector Machine (SVM with SMO) (Platt, 1998) classifier (both with 10-fold cross-validation) using separately the eigenvalues only, the linguistic features only, and the combination of both (denoted as *all*) (see Tables 2–5).

7.2 Best Features

We use the standard Information Gain (IG) feature selection algorithm (Peng et al., 2005) with 10-fold cross-validation to get the features that provide the most information gain with respect to class for each sub-corpus. Tables 2–5) summarize our experiments. While the best features for each sub-corpus are different, *Readability 1* (the one that does not include the idiom count) and *Word Count (WC)* appear in all 4 sets of best features. We then use the Readability 1 feature as the *only* feature to get classification results. Surprisingly, the Readability 1 feature alone achieves comparable classification accuracies as using all features we extract – 0.65, 0.65, 0.66, 0.54 respectively on the Bo Xilai, Kindergarten Abuse, Pollution & Food Safety, and Internet Censorship & Propaganda sub-corpus.

7.2.1 Readability and Word Count

The average readability score of all uncensored blogposts is higher than that of censored, i.e., uncensored blogposts on average are less difficult to read and understand. The average word count of all uncensored blogposts is higher than that of censored (i.e. uncensored blogposts on average are longer). The higher readability score of uncensored blogposts goes along with our hypothesis that uncensored blogposts tend to be easier to read. The higher readability score of uncensored blogposts also suggests that censored content could be semantically less straightforward and/or use more uncommon words. As microbloggers are aware of the possibility of censorship when discussing sensitive topics, various linguistic techniques might have been adopted such as satire as suggested by Lee (2016) and homophones as suggested by Hiruncharoenvate et. al (2015). Text readability decreases as microbloggers try to evade censorship. It

Features	Acc	Censored Pre	Censored Rec	Censored F1	Uncensored Pre	Uncensored Rec	Uncensored F1
NB all (147)	0.66	0.60	0.76	0.67	0.74	0.57	0.64
NB eigenvalues (40)	0.55	0.52	0.65	0.58	0.60	0.47	0.52
NB ling. features (107)	0.64	0.62	0.62	0.62	0.66	0.66	0.66
NB best features(33)	0.65	0.65	0.59	0.62	0.66	0.71	0.68
SMO all (147)	0.66	0.63	0.65	0.64	0.68	0.67	0.67
SMO eigenvalues (40)	0.56	0.55	0.40	0.46	0.57	0.70	0.63
SMO ling. features (107)	0.63	0.61	0.61	0.61	0.65	0.66	0.65
SMO best features (33)	0.67	0.64	0.66	0.65	0.67	0.67	0.67
majority class	0.53						

Table 5: Classification results for the Internet & Propaganda subcorpus.

Features	Acc	Censored Pre	Censored Rec	Censored F1	Uncensored Pre	Uncensored Rec	Uncensored F1
SMO (All features (148))	0.64	0.63	0.58	0.60	0.65	0.69	0.67
readability 1 (1)	0.51	0.43	0.11	0.17	0.52	0.88	0.65
readability 2 (1)	0.53	0.46	0.02	0.04	0.53	0.98	0.69
best features (82)	0.66	0.65	0.56	0.61	0.65	0.73	0.69
Majority Class	0.53						

Table 6: Linear SVM Classification results for the censorship corpus. All sub-corpora combined together.

is interesting to note that we do include each component of our readability metric (character frequency, word frequency and word count to semantic groups ratio) as an individual feature for the classifiers but they do not top the best features.

While the length of a text alone does not directly indicate readability, there might be implications when a longer blogpost is posted on a social media or microblog platform, where short texts are the norm.While a longer blogpost does not guarantee readership, it might invite more attention when users are browsing among other relatively short texts. One of the explanations why long and easy to read blogposts are deliberately left untouched by the censors is that these posts are expected to impact the readers' opinions as is predicted by Schwarz et al. (2008) who claim that easier materials are more influential to readers.

8 Discussion

To get a better understanding of the language differences between censored and uncensored text and what words are associated with what class, we subtract the average percentage of words in each feature from the best feature set in the censored posts from their corresponding uncensored values. A positive result indicates an association between a feature and the uncensored class, whereas a negative result indicates an association between a feature and the censored class. We find that the use of third person plural pronoun ('they'), swear words ('fuck', 'damn', 'shit' etc.), and words that express anger ('hate', 'annoyed', 'kill' etc.) and certainty ('always', 'never' etc.) are more associated with censored blogposts across all 4 sub-corpora, whereas interrogatives ('how', 'when', 'what' etc.), the Internet slang ('lol', 'plz', 'thx' etc.), and words that talk about the present ('today', 'now' etc.), sadness ('crying', 'grief' etc.) and vision ('view', 'see' etc.) are more associated with the uncensored blogposts for all 4 sub-corpora. This suggests that blogposts that express opinions in a furious, cursing manner and with certainty might be more susceptible to censorship, while blogposts that are more casual and appealing (the heavier use of Internet Slangs), more focused on discussing or querying the current state of matter (interrogatives, present words, and vision words), or describe negative emotion in a less intimidating way are tend to left uncensored. In a sense, by not blocking this type of posts, the censors provide an outlet for the bloggers to express their criticism and negative emotions without growing angry, since anger might lead to action.

While we do not explicitly experiment on collective action potential (CAP) proposed by King et al. (2013), some of our findings show characteristics common with CAP – social engagement. According to Pennebaker et al. (2015), "third person pronouns are, by definition, markers to suggest that the speaker is socially engaged or aware." Generally, the features typical of censored content convey social engagement, confidence and anger, and involve fewer words that refer to senses, but more words that describe cognitive processes. This finding also goes along with our hypothesis that censored and uncensored texts each has their own unique linguistic characteristics.

Although incorporating idioms in the readability metrics does not improve the performance of the models on the merged corpus, we noticed a slight improvement in the performance of the classifier on the Pollution & Environment and the Internet Censorship sub-corpora. The normalized idiom count are selected as one of the best features for these two datasets. It is worth noting that 39% and 22% of censored and uncensored blogposts respectively contain idioms overall, and that idioms are negatively correlated with the Readability 1 score. For the Pollution & Environment and the Internet Censorship sub-corpora, the differences in the usage of idioms between the censored and uncensored classes are more prominent. It is yet to be investigated in what other ways idioms might contribute to the prediction of censorship and how to incorporate them into the model.

9 Limitations

Since we compare censored and uncensored data that share the same keyword(s) in their textual content, and due to the fact that the SinaWeibo does not allow more than 200 results to be returned from their keyword search API, our data is collected manually and therefore the quantity is not large. Also, our censored data source does not necessarily track the publishing history of every single SinaWeibo user. Our goal is to further improve the representativeness of our data in future work. Although Bamman et al. (2012) has shown the geographical differences in censorship rate of blogposts, our concern is on textual content only. It is possible that some fine-grained linguistic differences might exist in censored data due to geographical differences. However, this is left for future work to gauge such patterns, if they exist.

10 Conclusion

We described a pilot study in which we built a model to classify censored and uncensored social media posts from mainland China. We deliberately did not use topics as classification features because some censorable topics vary throughout time and across countries, but linguistic fingerprints should not. Our goal is to explore whether linguistic features could be effective in discriminating between censored and uncensored content. We have found such features that characterize the two categories and built classifiers that achieve promising results. The focus of this study is on censorship in mainland China. However, there are many other regions around the world that exercise Internet censorship. It is important to verify if the features we identified hold cross-linguistically.

Acknowledgements

We thank the anonymous reviewers for their careful reading of this article and their many insightful comments and suggestions. This work is supported by the National Science Foundation under Grant No.: 1704113, Division of Computer and Networked Systems, Secure & Trustworthy Cyberspace (SaTC).

References

David Bamman, Brendan O'Connor, and Noah A. Smith. 2012. Censorship and deletion practices in chinese social media. *First Monday*, 17(3).

Jacob Cohen. 1960. A Coefficient of Agreement for Nominal Scales. *Education and Psychological Measurement*, (20):37–46.

Jun Da. 2004. Title: A corpus-based study of character and bigram frequencies in chinese e-texts and its implications for chinese language instruction. In Pu Zhang, Xie Tianwei, and Juan Xu, editors, *The studies on the theory and methodology of the digitalized Chinese teaching to foreigners: Proceedings of the Fourth International Conference on New Technologies in Teaching and Learning Chinese.*, pages 501–511. Beijing: Tsinghua University Press.

Chaya Hiruncharoenvate, Zhiyuan Lin, and Eric Gilbert. 2015. Algorithmically bypassing censorship on sina weibo with nondeterministic homophone substitutions. In *Ninth International AAAI Conference on Web and Social Media.*

Chin-Lan Huang, Cindy Chung, Natalie K. Hui, Yi-Cheng Lin, Yi-Tai Seih, Ben C.P. Lam, Wei-Chuan Chen, Michael Bond, and James H. Pennebaker. 2012. The development of the chinese linguistic inquiry and word count dictionary. *Chinese Journal of Psychology*, 54(2):185–201.

jiā jū Méi. 1984. *The Chinese Thesaurus.*

George H. John and Pat Langley. 1995. Estimating continuous distributions in bayesian classifiers. In *Eleventh Conference on Uncertainty in Artificial Intelligence*, pages 338–345, San Mateo. Morgan Kaufmann.

S. Katti, D. Katabi, and K. Puchala. 2005. Slicing the onion: Anonymous routing without pki. Technical report, MIT CSAIL Technical Report 1000.

Gary King, Jennifer Pan, and Margaret E Roberts. 2013. How censorship in china allows government criticism but silences collective expression. *American Political Science Review*, 107(2):1–18, May.

J. Knockel, M. Crete-Nishihata, J.Q. Ng, A. Senft, and J.R. Crandall. 2015. Every rose has its thorn: Censorship and surveillance on social video platforms in china. In *Proceedings of the 5th USENIX Workshop on Free and Open Communications on the Internet.*

Christopher S. Leberknight, Mung Chiang, and Felix Ming Fai Wong. 2012. A taxonomy of censors and anti-censors: Part i-impacts of internet censorship. *International Journal of E-Politics (IJEP)*, 3(2).

S. Lee. 2016. Surviving online censorship in china: Three satirical tactics and their impact. *China Quarterly.*

D. Levin, Y. Lee, L.Valenta, Z. Li amd V. Lai, C. Lumezanu, N. Spring, and B. Bhattacharjee. 2015. Alibi routing. In *Proceedings of the 2015 ACM Conference on Special Interest Group on Data Communication.*

Stephan Lewandowsky, Ullrich K. H. Ecker, Colleen M. Seifert orbert Schwarz, and John Cook. 2012. Misinformation and its correction continued influence and successful debiasing. *Psychological Science in the Public Interest*, 13(3):106–131.

Richard McPherson, Reza Shokri, and Vitaly Shmatikov. 2016. Defeating image obfuscation with deep learning. arXiv preprint arXiv:1609.00408.

Tomas Mikolov, Kai Chen, Greg Corrado, and Jeffrey Dean. 2013a. Efficient estimation of word representations in vector space. In *Proceedings of Workshop at ICLR.*

Tomas Mikolov, Ilya Sutskever, Kai Chen, Greg Corrado, and Jeffrey Dean. 2013b. Distributed representations of words and phrases and their compositionality. In *Proceedings of NIPS.*

H. Peng, F. Long, and C. Ding. 2005. Feature selection based on mutual information criteria of max-dependency, max-relevance, and min-redundancy. *EEE Transactions Pattern Analysis and Machine Intelligence*, 27(8):1226–1238.

James W. Pennebaker, Ryan L. Boyd, Kayla Jordan, and Kate Blackburn. 2015. The development and psychometric the development of psychometric properties of liwc. Technical report, University of Texas at Austin.

James W. Pennebaker, Roger Booth, and M.E. Francis, 2017. *Linguistic Inquiry and Word Count (LIWC2007).*

John Platt. 1998. Fast training of support vector machines using sequential minimal optimization. In *Advances in Kernel Methods - Support Vector Learning*. MIT Press, January.

Iris Safaka, Christina Fragouli, , and Katerina Argyraki. 2016. Matryoshka: Hiding secret communication in plain sight. In *6th USENIX Workshop on Free and Open Communications on the Internet (FOCI 16). USENIX Association.*

Anthony W. Sali, Brian A. Anderson, and Susan M. Courtney. 2016. Information processing biases in the brain: Implications for decision-making and self-governance. *NeuroEthics*, pages 1–13.

Norbert Schwarz, Hyunjin Song, and Jing Xu, 2008. *When thinking is difficult: Metacognitive experiences as information*, pages 201–223. Psychology Press, 12.

Y.T. Sung, T.H. Chang, W.C. Lin, K.S. Hsieh, and K.E. Chang. 2015. Crie: An automated analyzer for chinese texts. *Behavior Research Method.*

L. Tang and P. Yang. 2011. Symbolic power and the internet: The power of a 'horse'. *Media, Culture & Society*, 33(5):675–691.

S Wang. 2012. China's internet lexicon: The symbolic meaning and commoditization of grass mud horse in the harmonious society. *First Monday*, 7(1-2).

Zachary Weinberg, Jeffrey Wang, Vinod Yegneswaran, Linda Briesemeister, Steven Cheung, Frank Wang, and Dan Boneh. 2012. Stegotorus: A camouflage proxy for the tor anonymity system. *Proceedings of the 19th ACM conference on Computer and Communications Security.*

Jinquan Zheng. 2005. Cíhuì yǔyì yǔ jùzi yuèdú nányì dù jìliàng. In *The 6th Chinese Lexical Semantic Workshop Title:.*

T. Zhu, D. Phipps, A. Pridgen, JR Crandall, and DS Wallach. 2013. The velocity of censorship: high-fidelity detection of microblog post deletions. arXiv:1303.0597 [cs.CY].

Creative Language Encoding under Censorship

Heng Ji
Rensselaer Polytechnic Institute
jih@rpi.edu

Kevin Knight
University of Southern California
knight@isi.edu

Abstract

People often create obfuscated language for online communication to avoid Internet censorship, share sensitive information, express strong sentiment or emotion, plan for secret actions, trade illegal products, or simply hold interesting conversations. In this position paper we systematically categorize human-created obfuscated language on various levels, investigate their basic mechanisms, give an overview on automated techniques needed to simulate human encoding. These encoders have potential to frustrate and evade, co-evolve with dynamic human or automated decoders, and produce interesting and adoptable code words. We also summarize remaining challenges for future research on the interaction between Natural Language Processing (NLP) and encryption, and leveraging NLP techniques for encoding and decoding.

1 Introduction

According to a recent study by Freedom on the Net[1], 67% of netizens live in countries where criticism of the government, military, or ruling family is subject to censorship. For example, censorship on Chinese social media is intensive (Chen et al., 2013; Zhu et al., 2013; King et al., 2014; Hiruncharoenvate et al., 2015). Users must register with their real identities (name, social security number, address, phone number and email). Social media platforms temporarily shut down commenting functions or remove user accounts. One part of the censorship is conducted via maintaining and updating a list of blacklisted keywords [2] to block certain known code words. This aggressive censorship mechanism also produces false alarms and filters regular posts. For example, on July 22, 2012, a heavy rainstorm in Beijing killed 77 people partially due to the slow response from the government. General terms such as 事故 *(accident)* were added into the blacklisted word lists, and thus all posts about any accidents were removed. As another example, on April 20, 2018, a popular humorous video app *Neihan Duanzi* with more than 100 million users was permanently shut down. Angered by the closure, many protests organized online as flash-mobs, using secret signals to allow *Duanzi friends* to recognize each other: a car-horn beeped in a specific long-short-short rhythm *Di...di di*, a double-flash of the headlights, and a coded song sung at the same time across the country by replacing 孤立墙 *(isolated wall)* with 柏林墙 *(Berlin wall)*, 艳阳雪 *(sunshine and snow)* with 六月雪 *(snow fell in June, an idiom that indicates injustice)*.

In this paper we overview how humans and machines encode intent into appropriate, interesting, and adoptable language to enable netizens to evade censorship and freely communicate with general netizens. These techniques attack a fundamentally challenging problem in automatically understanding fast-evolving social media language, especially for netizens without culture-specific knowledge. Coded words have made human language evolve faster than ever, on a daily basis, due to the tension between encoding and decoding objectives. This opens an unexplored area of coded language processing.

[1] https://freedomhouse.org/report/freedom-net/freedom-net-2016
[2] https://en.wikipedia.org/wiki/Internet_censorship_in_China

Proceedings of the First Workshop on Natural Language Processing for Internet Freedom, pages 23–33
Santa Fe, New Mexico, USA, August 20, 2018.

2 Human Encoding

2.1 Categories of Coded Language

Netizens create and use obfuscated language for a variety of purposes.

Discussing sensitive information and evading censorship. Code words widely exist in Chinese social media (Huang et al., 2013; Zhang et al., 2014; Zhang et al., 2015). Bamman et al. (2012) automatically discover politically sensitive terms from Chinese tweets based on message deletion analysis. When Chinese netizens talk about the former politician 周永康 *(Zhou Yongkang)*, they use a coded word 康师傅 *(Master Kang)*, a brand of instant noodles whose Chinese spellings share one character 康 *(kang)*. The Enron emails[3] also include many code words, such as *dinosaur* referring to an illegal stock.

Masking illegal activity. In the dark web for human trafficking, arms dealing, and drug dealing, *research chemical* or *RC* is euphemistically used to discuss psychoactive chemicals that are not yet scheduled as narcotics. *ice* and *skiing* refer to *Cocaine*. Phone numbers are often obfuscated (e.g. *7o2 7two7 7four87, four-oh-eight 9OO-one*) (Szekely et al., 2015).

Terror plots. Terrorists often use seemingly innocent conversations laced with coded messages and double-speak. 9/11 attacker Abu Abdul Rahman told accomplice Ramzi Binalshibh in an Internet chat room: *To German girlfriend: The first semester commences in three weeks. Two high schools and two universities... This summer will surely be hot ... 19 certificates for private education and four exams. Regards to the professor. Goodbye.*[4] Here, *in three weeks* refers to *September 11, 2011*, *two high schools* refers to *World Trade Center*, *the professor* refers to *Bin Laden*, *19 certificates* means *19 hijackers* and *four exams* means *four planes*, etc.. In addition, three targets bear a code name. The US Capitol building was called *The Faculty of Law*; the Pentagon became *The Faculty of Fine Arts*; and the North Tower of the World Trade Center was code-named as *The Faculty of Town Planning*. Table 1 lists more examples of seemingly innocuous terms which are terror code words and their meanings, based on reports from FBI and the International Center for Political Violence and Terrorism Research in Singapore[5][6][7].

Code Word	Meaning
peanut butter, wedding, jelly sandwich	terrorist attacks
culinary school	training camps
rap concert	a training run before an attack
rash, skin disease	under surveillance
eggplant	rocket-propelled grenade
tourism, smelling fresh air, warehouse	taking part in jihad
little girl	terrorist
Abid Naseer's girlfriend Nadia	bomb
banana, creps (Nike trainers)	firearm
cheese	money
iron	weapons
football, soccer	fighting
get married	to be killed
Brian, Bob	FBI agents
land of the two rivers	Iraq
P-town	Pakistan

Table 1: Examples of Terror Code Words

[3]https://en.wikipedia.org/wiki/Enron_Corpus

[4]https://en.wikipedia.org/wiki/Ramzi_bin_al-Shibh

[5]http://insider.foxnews.com/2014/09/20/inside-language-terrorism-isis-code-words-include-pbj-rap-concert-and-rash

[6]https://www.reuters.com/article/us-usa-padilla/u-s-terrorism-trial-ponders-meaning-of-eggplant-idUSN0129968420070701

[7]https://nypost.com/2014/09/13/jihadi-tapes-reveal-sinister-pbj-code-in-culinary-school/

Plain slang in a particular domain, community, youth language, or cutesy language: In sports gambling, *getting down* means *placing a bet*. Japanese cartoon and game fans create many domain-specific code words: e.g., 電波 *(Radio wave)* refers to weird but charming characters who mind-control others by doing unexpected things. In teens' secret language, acronyms are widely used: *ABFL* means *a big fat lady*, and *POTS* means *parents over the shoulder*. Some code words are not used to conceal, but rather as trendy jargon, e.g., *ELI5* means *Explain Like I'm 5*.

Expressing strong emotion and sentiment, or making fun: Sometimes netizens encode fun and creative language to express sarcasm, irony statement, positive/negative sentiment, strong emotion, or vivid descriptions of entities and events. 剁手党 *(hand-chopping party)* refers to a group of people who are addicted to online shopping. The majority regret their shopping sprees and vow in vain to chop off their hands should they spend their money so easily again.

2.2 Challenges for Decoding

These kinds of coded language present challenges for censorship:

Synonymy and Polysemy. Mature information extraction techniques can extract and resolve entities and events from text. However, coded language defeats most contextual features used by these techniques. Less-mature metaphor detection (Wang et al., 2006; Tsvetkov, 2013; Heintz et al., 2013) techniques also have trouble with abstract coded language. Word-sense disambiguation techniques (Yarowsky, 1995; Mihalcea, 2007; Navigli, 2009) deal in sense inventories that are fairly static over time, whereas code language evolves rapidly.

Large number of candidates. Coded language effectively hides in plain sight because anything can be a candidate to the decoder. It is challenging to discover code words from social media text because less than 3% unique terms are code words (Zhang et al., 2015). Moreover, common words and phrases are often used as code words to avoid censorship. For example, 姐夫 *(jie fu)* can be used to refer to both its literal meaning *brother-in-law* or the Russian politician Medvedev whose name's Chinese transliteration ends with syllables that have similar pronunciations as *jie fu*. Likewise it is difficult to resolve to real targets after they are identified. Entity Linking techniques such as (Pan et al., 2015) resolve entity ambiguity by linking mentions to an external knowledge base (KB), while there is no existing KB that covers a wide range of target entities, implicit concepts and events referred by code words.

Lack of labeled data. No sufficient mention-level code annotations exist for training an end-to-end encoder or decoder. Manual code annotations require native speakers who have cultural background (Zhang et al., 2014), so novel approaches are needed to save annotation cost.

Lack of background knowledge for the target concepts and stories. 薄熙来 *(Bo Xilai)* , a former Chinese politician, was found guilty of corruption, stripped of all his assets, and sentenced to life imprisonment. In Chinese social media Bo is coded as 平西王 *(Conquer West King)* who was a historical figure four hundreds years ago who governed the same region as Bo and also suffered from a downfall and an arrest at the end of his career. 真红女王 *(Truly Red Queen)* is a main character in Rozen Maiden, a Japanese manga series. It is used as a code name for 江青 *(Jiang Qing)*, a major political figure during the Cultural Revolution by Chinese Communist Party; because the color red is associated with communism, and she was the fourth wife of Mao Zedong, the first Chairman of China (*queen*).

2.3 Entity Encoding

Zhang et al. (2014) did a preliminary study on categorizing methods to create code words that refer to entities. The surface forms of human created code words usually appear quite different from their target names. 26% of human encoded entity mentions are based on the entity's reputation and public perception, and 21% of them are based on modeling the entity's characteristics. According to (Zhang et al., 2013), in 1,500 randomly sampled tweets that include 10,098 unique terms, there are 1,342 coded mentions that refer to 250 unique entities. Some frequent code word examples from Reddit[8] and Sina Weibo[9], a

[8]https://www.reddit.com/

[9]https://weibo.com

China-based microblogging platform, are presented in Table 2.

Code Word	Target Entity	Comment
苏牙 (Su-tooth)	Luis Suarez	Luis Suarez bites other players.
康敏苏小姐 (Miss Coming Soon)	Lady Gaga	Lady Gaga said that her "Do What You Want" MV was coming soon several times around five years ago but it has not been released yet.
邓黑猫 (Deng Black Cat)	邓小平 (Deng Xiaoping)	*Black Cat* originates from Deng Xiaoping's famous quote: "No matter white or black, a cat that catches mice is a good cat".
Indian Hay	cannabis	from India
Jelly Bean	amphetamine	similar shape
Jelly Green	marijuana	similar color
Ice, Lady Snow	cocaine	similar appearance

Table 2: Examples of Attribute-based Code Words

Many human-created code words are based on domain mapping, done in a consistent and memorable way. Table 3 and Table 4 present some examples. From these examples we can see that the most popular code domains are food, celebrity, animal, and cartoon. These code words tend to be innocent, cute, vivid, impressive, and easy to remember. The incongruity theory (Mulder and Nijholt, 2002) states that humor is perceived at the moment of realization of incongruity between a concept involved in a certain situation and the real objects thought to be in some relation to the concept. Code words created by domain mapping naturally match this theory because of the domain shifts between code words and the contexts. For example, *kiwi* is the most popular code word referring to Chris Evans, due to his bearded face. So a post like "kiwi took off his shoes!" is funnier than "Chris took off his shoes!". Many code words are created based on archetypes, i.e., innate, universal prototypes. When such prototypes can be observed among celebrities, their names will be directly used as code words. For example, 楚霸王 *(Xiangyu, king of western Chu)* is often used to refer to brave people. When no proper names could be easily found to represent a prototype, a new code name will be created. For example, 朝阳群众 *(The people of Chaoyang district)* refers to anonymous volunteer security patrols in Beijing. They began to gain fame on social media after being credited by police as leading to the arrests of several celebrities involved in drug-related crimes.

When using the domain-mapping strategy, code words in the same thread tend to be consistently derived from the same domain, and thus they are topically coherent. For instance, in a thread when *ice* is used to refer to *methylamphetamine*, then ice or snow related code words will be used for other drugs (e.g., *Lady Snow* for *cocaine*) and actions (*ice cream habit* for *occasional use of drugs*). In contrast, when *juice* is used to refer to drugs, then *Pepsi habit* will be used instead. Similarly when animals are used to refer to drugs, then *chicken scratching* and *henpicking* are used to describe a crack addict searching on their hands and knees for drugs; and *bulls* instead of the more common *Big John* will be used to refer to the police.

2.4 Story Encoding

Obfuscated language is also used to encode an entire paragraph, especially for planning certain activities. For example, North Korean people changed the well-known rhythm song "*Three Bears*" to include satirical references to the Kim family dynasty:

- **Original version:** *Three bears in a house, papa bear, mama bear and baby bear. Papa Bear is fat, Mama Bear is thin, Baby Bear is too cute.*

Code	Code Domain	Target	Shared Characteristics
lemon, lemonade	food	poor quality drugs	light, ineffective
lettuce	innocent items	cash money	cheap items
wild cat	animal	methcathinone	methcathinone's spelling includes *cat*, strong effect (*wild*).
Jane, Jay, Juanita, Aunt Mary	common person name	marijuana	rhyming slang
King	common, person name	cocaine	rhyming slang
Jimmy	celebrity	the foil used when smoking heroin	*foil* is a rhyming slang for *Boyle* in Jimmy Boyle
Kate Bush	celebrity	Kind Bud	*Kind* is pronounced *Kine* in its origin Hawaii, which means *excellent*
Jefferson Airplane	celebrity	used match cut in half to hold a partially smoked marijuana cigarette	Jefferson Airplane was split into the two bands
LBJ	celebrity	LSD, PCP and heroin	LBJ is best known as the initials of former US president Lyndon, Baines and Johnson
420	song	marijuana	420 = 12*35, Bob Dylan's song "Rainy Day Woman #12 and 35" has a line "Everybody Must Get Stoned" which is mistakenly associated with smoking marijuana
Snow White	cartoon	cocaine	similar appearance with snow flake
Peter Pan	cartoon	PCP	similar abbreviations
Tina	TV series	crystal methamphetamine	Molly Meade is a character in "Ugly Betty", *Molly Meade* is rhyming slang for *methamphetamine* and *Tina* is created to represent as Molly's ugly and meaner (*crystal*) sister.

Table 3: Domain Mapping Examples for Drug Dealing

- **Modified version:** Three bears in a house, **pocketing everything**; **grandpa** bear, papa bear and baby bear. **Grandpa** Bear is **fat**, Papa Bear is fat, too, and Baby Bear is a **doofus**.

Chinese netizens sometimes need to encode a whole story in order to express politically-sensitive ideas. For example, a thread about the arrest of Bo Xilai was initiated by a coded post and then replied to by another post using code words from the same food domain (nine contestants refer to the nine members of the CCP Standing Committee):

- **Initial Post:** *A few days ago, Beijing was hosting an innovative* ***tug-of-war*** *for* ***the elderly; this game*** *has* ***nine contestants*** *in all.* ***The first round*** *of the contest is still intense ···* ***The teletubby team*** *noticeably has the advantage and, relatively,* ***the Master Kang team*** *is obviously falling short.*
- **Reply Post:** ***Tomato*** *has retreated; what* ***flavour*** *will* ***Master Kang*** *still have?*

The idea of story encoding is not new. Many classic English nursery rhymes were started as 19th-century "blog posts" criticizing British government figures. It can be further traced back to the tradition of writing acrostic poems and articles in ancient China.

Code	Code Domain	Target	Target Domain	Shared Characteristics
西红柿 (tomato)	vegetable	Chongqing City	politics	tomato is a homonym for 西红市 *(western red city)*; Chongqing, the largest city in China's southwest, was the front line of the red revival.
Black Mamba	animal	Kobe Bryant	sports	venomous, agile, aggressive.
silver fox	animal	Anderson Cooper	celebrity	gray hair, handsome, wise, attractive
黄金脆皮鹅 (Golden Crispy Goose)	animal	Lady Gaga	celebrity	Lady Gaga dressed up like a goose in her "Applause" MV and "G.U.Y." MV.
轮胎 (tire)	product	胡锦涛 (Hu Jintao)	politics	锦湖 (Jin Hu) is Chinese translation of South Korean tire brand *Kumho*; which can be read in reverse as the first two characters of *Hu Jintao*'s name.
Angel	historical book	Air Force One	terrorism	Angel was used extensively for Air Force One throughout William Manchester's 1967 book, "The Death Of A President".
古月 (Gu Yue)	drama	胡锦涛 (Hu Jintao)	politics	the first character of 胡锦涛 can be decomposed into two characters 古月; and 古月 is a famous actor playing Mao Zedong. Both Mao and Hu acted as the former chairman of China.

Table 4: Domain Mapping Examples for Other Purposes

3 System Encoding and Decoding

3.1 Cipher for Encoding

Traditional text encryption techniques focus on alphabetic substitution or transposition based on lexical level (Franceschini and Mukherjee, 1996; Venkateswaran and Sundaram, 2010), synonyms (Chang and Clark, 2014) or image-adaptive public watermarking (Sun et al., 2008). Cipher systems can also be potentially developed and mutated to encode messages, including compare sophisticated ciphers such as historical ones (Knight et al., 2011) and simple mutations such as Leet[10] and Martian script[11]. Further strategies need to be developed to make them easy and fun for target human comprehension and widespread adoption, and difficult for automatic decoding.

3.2 Natural Language Generation for Encoding

Knight and Hatzivassiloglou (1995) and Langkilde and Knight (1998) lay the foundation for statistical natural language generation, and they recently apply these techniques to the generation of creative language:

(1) **Portmanteau neologism creation.** They fuse existing English words to create novel ones (Deri and Knight, 2015). The aim is to create an amusing new form that is understandable by a reader, e.g., *frenemy* for an entity that is both *friend* and *enemy*. Doing this well requires fusion at the phonetic level followed by an appropriate choice of spelling. Machines cannot yet process such created neologisms. This portmanteau generation approach (Deri and Knight, 2015) can be used to encode other types of neologisms

[10]https://en.wikipedia.org/wiki/Leet

[11]https://en.wikipedia.org/wiki/Martian_language

in both English and Chinese. We observe the words embedded are usually semantically and phonetically compatible, such as "*frenemy (friend + enemy)*". They are also terse, representative, expressive, interesting and easy to remember. For example, the following short phrases are created to refer to good men and bad men respectively: "暖男 *(warm + man)*" and "渣男 *(dirt + man)*".

(2) **Dynamic phrasebooks.** Tourists frequently carry phonetic phrasebooks that allow them to say things in a language they do not know. In (Shi et al., 2014), we developed a system that accepts text entered by a user (e.g., Chinese), translates the text (e.g., into English), then converts the translation into a phonetic spelling in the user's own orthography (e.g., Chinese). This system let users say anything they want, even if it is not in any phrasebook, using their own voice. For example, if a Chinese visitor to the United States wants to say 早上好 (meaning *Good morning*), they enter this phrase, and the system tells them to instead say 古德莫宁 (pronounced *gu-de-mo-ning*). This user is not required to know any English, but can still be understood by monolingual English speakers. This technique can be applied for encoding with the following two improvements: (1) replace human translation with machine translation (MT) to make the results more challenging to decode because it is difficult to recover from MT errors, and (2) polish the output by using common words or phrases in the user's own orthography, so the coded messages are more easily remembered and adopted. An encoded message is as follows.

- **Chinese**: 明天下午三点到鼓楼大街集合。
- **English translation**: Let's gather at the Bell Tower Street at 3pm tomorrow.
- **Pronounce English in Chinese phonetic system (pinyin)**: Laici galete ate de beier taoer sijute aite teli piaimu temoluo.
- **Code by spelling out pinyin**: 来此盖乐特爱特得贝尔套儿思聚特爱特特例皮埃姆特摩罗。

(3) **Poetry passwords.** (Greene et al., 2010) build the first statistical machine translation system to translate poetry. They subsequently apply poetry generation techniques to the problem of password security (Ghazvininejad and Knight, 2015). In this work, the machine first assigns a random 60-bit password to a user. Because the user cannot remember a random sequence of 0's and 1's, the machine converts the bit sequence into a more memorable iambic tetrameter couplet (e.g., *The legendary Japanese // subsidiaries overseas*). The mapping between bit sequences and poems is reversible, so the security of the randomly-assigned password is maintained.

Brennan et al. (2012) propose three methods to create adversarial passages: obfuscation, imitation, and translation. They find manual circumvention methods work very well, while automated translation methods are not effective. Potash et al. (2015) develop a *GhostWriter* system that can take a given artist's rap lyrics and generate similar yet unique lyrics. Other recent work detects word obfuscation in adversarial communication (Roussinov et al., 2007; Fong et al., 2008; Jabbari et al., 2008; Deshmukh et al., 2014; Agarwal and Sureka, 2015) using existing commonsense KBs such as ConceptNet (Agarwal and Sureka, 2015).

3.3 Entity Encoding and Decoding

Huang et al. (2013), Zhang et al. (2014) and Zhang et al. (2015) study a problem of encoding and decoding *entity morph*, which is a special case of coded name alias to hide the original entities for expressing strong sentiment or evading censorship in Chinese social media. They propose a variety of novel approaches to automatically encode proper and interesting morphs (Zhang et al., 2014), including Phonetic Substitution, Spelling Decomposition, Nickname Generation, Translation and Transliteration and Historical Figure Mapping, which can effectively pass decoding tests. They also develop an effective morph decoder, which can automatically identify and resolve entity morphs to their real targets (Huang et al., 2013; Zhang et al., 2015) and released manually annotated data sets for encoding[12] and decoding[13] experiments. They capture implicit attributes of entities using word embeddings. For example, they automatically encode 姚明 *(Yao Ming)* as 姚奇才 *(Yao Wizard)*. However, this simple approach based on general distributional semantics only receives 52% overall human satisfaction rate, which is significantly lower than that of human encoding methods (77%). They found that human methods are much better than automatic methods

[12]http://nlp.cs.rpi.edu/data/morphencoding.tar.gz

[13]http://nlp.cs.rpi.edu/data/morphdecoding.zip

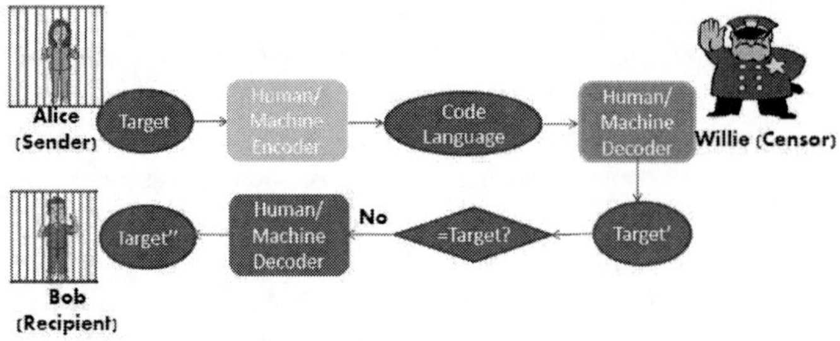

Figure 1: Encoding and Decoding as Prisoners Problem

at quickly picking up the best attributes for encoding, as well as connecting dots (seemingly irrelevant attributes) for decoding.

4 Remaining Problems

Many interesting challenges remain to be explored for effective creative language encoding.

Prisoners Problem: The first basic goal is to make sure the target human receiver (e.g., Bob in Figure 1) can successfully receive and decode the code words from the sender (Alice) by passing the censor (Willie). Creative language is used to communicate confidential information without encryption. Shannon's maxim "the enemy knows the system" does not always hold. There is usually no chance for the sender and the potential recipient to agree on a common code-book or secret key in advance. A smart encoder should go far beyond surface changes on spellings or pronunciations. It must be on-topic, containing clues for a human receiver to understand without specialized background knowledge.

Representative: Code words should be unique, expressive, discriminative, vivid to indicate what the target is well-known for, and easy to remember. For example, *Kimchi Country* is a good code name for South Korea. Terror code words often use the names of fruits and vegetables for weapons of similar shapes. (Lin et al., 2015) ranked the attributes in a typical human created knowledge base based on how well each attribute can distinguish entities. The top ranked ones include a person's social security number or an organization's website. However, such attributes will be easily caught by an automatic decoder. The good attributes do not necessarily appear very frequently either. They must be up-to-date for a certain burst event, topic, life snapshot, domain, or reputation during a certain time period.

Adoptable: Zhang et al. (2015) shows human created code words are considered as funnier (76% satisfaction rate) than machine created ones (46% satisfaction rate), which make them more impressive and adoptable for future use. For example, the character 牙 *(tooth)* in the code word for "*Luis Suarez*" in Table 2 is funny because it indicates his unusual habit of biting. The ultimate goal of encoding is to disseminate code words widely so they can become part of the new Internet language. Zhang et al. (2014) showed that popular code words tend to include unusual combinations of characters or words, negative sentiment and sarcasm, and they are usually simple, cute and easy to remember. However, a deeper and more comprehensive categorization and analysis on human created code words is required to formally extract their representative criteria for automated encoders to follow.

Time-sensitivity: Figure 2 shows the code frequency change for targets Bo Xilai at Sina Weibo. We can see the drops in the frequency of code words around sensitive dates (June 4, the anniversary of Tiananmen Square protests of 1989[14], etc). The censorship system is highly flexible. Certain code words may be blocked during politically-sensitive periods of the year, while others may be blacklisted for just a short time due to some contemporary relevant issue. Therefore, code words need to rapidly co-evolve with machine or human decoder over time, as some code words are discovered and blocked by censorship and newly created code words emerge. To fully automate human encoding approaches, a never-ending

[14] https://en.wikipedia.org/wiki/Tiananmen_Square_protests_of_1989

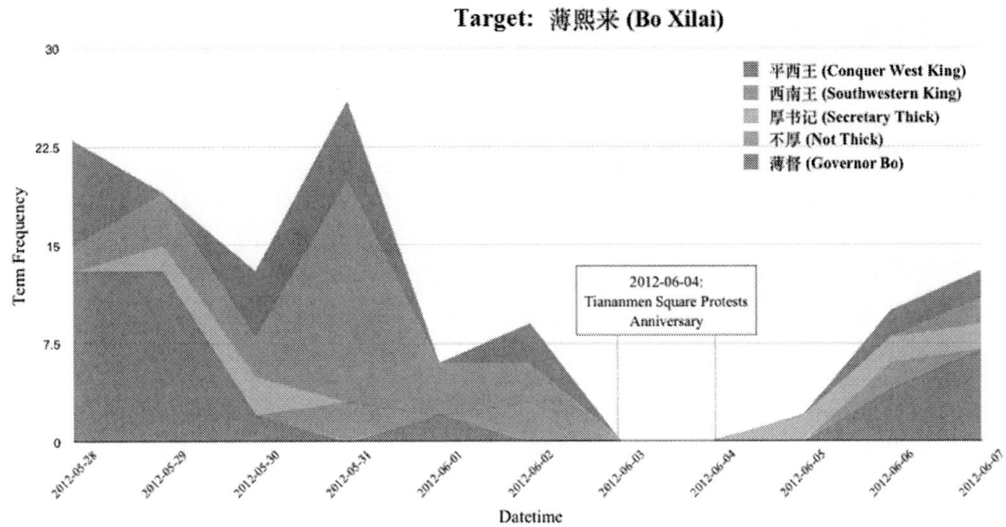

Figure 2: Code Frequency Change at Sina Weibo

learning component is needed to discover and select novel, salient and anomaly entities and events, update their profiles over time, rank and select the most discriminative characteristics of the targets for encoding.

Personalization: Most of the measures above are user-subjective. An ideal encoder should act as a friend instead of a servant or a co-worker. It should be a user-oriented, real-time, interactive encoding framework customized for both the sender and the receiver. The encoder should also incorporate the target reader's cultural background and psychological traits (gender, origin, education, moral value, power, belief, religion, social norm, current interests, culture, sense of humor, work intensity, etc), as recognized by user profile, social network information, target log history, previous posts, location, and time, into the encoder's short-term memory.

Multi-lingual: As we see from examples in English and Chinese, different encoding strategies can be developed for different writing systems. Another interesting research problems is to extend encoding methods to a wide range of languages which represent different writing systems and cover a large proportion of the world's population, including Latin, Cyrillic, Arabic, Devanagari, and Hangul scripts, as well as other languages in countries and regions with Internet censorship such as Arabic, Burmese, Farsi, Russian, Turkish, Uyghur, Urdu, and Vietnamese.

5 Conclusions

We summarized the current status and remaining challenges for a new and important research area of creative language encoding under censorship. Such encoding tools, if successful, will also be able to fast co-evolve over time with the semi-automatic censorship system' own evolutionary processes and ultimately defeat it. In the meanwhile it will bring new challenges and opportunities for adapting downstream natural language processing techniques to understand coded languages.

References

Swati Agarwal and Ashish Sureka. 2015. Using common-sense knowledge-base for detecting word obfuscation in adversarial communication. In *Proc. COMSNETS*.

David Bamman, Brendan O'Connor, and Noah A. Smith. 2012. Censorship and deletion practices in Chinese social media. *First Monday*, 17(3).

Michael Brennan, Sadia Afroz, and Rachel Greenstadt. 2012. Adversarial stylometry: Circumventing authorship recognition to preserve privacy and anonymity. *ACM Transactions on Information and System Security*, 15.

Ching-Yun Chang and Stephen Clark. 2014. Practical linguistic steganography using contextual synonym substitution and a novel vertex coding method. *Computational Linguistics*.

Le Chen, Chi Zhang, and Christo Wilson. 2013. Tweeting under pressure: Analyzing trending topics and evolving word choice on Sina Weibo. In *Proc. the first ACM conference on Online social networks*.

Aliya Deri and Kevin Knight. 2015. How to make a frenemy: Multitape FSTs for portmanteau generation. In *Proc. NAACL-HLT*.

Sonal N. Deshmukh, Ratnadeep R. Deshmukh, and Sachin N. Deshmukh. 2014. Performance analysis of different sentence oddity measures applied on Google and Google News repository for detection of substitution. *IRJES*, 3(3).

SzeWang Fong, Dmitri Roussinov, and David B. Skillicorn. 2008. Detecting word substitutions in text. *IEEE Transactions on Knowledge and Data Engineering*, 20(8).

Robert Franceschini and Amar Mukherjee. 1996. Data compression using encrypted text. In *Proc. IEEE Data Compression Conference*.

Marjan Ghazvininejad and Kevin Knight. 2015. How to memorize a random 60-bit string. In *Proc. NAACL-HLT*.

Erica Greene, Tugba Bodrumlu, and Kevin Knight. 2010. Automatic analysis of rhythmic poetry with applications to generation and translation. In *Proc. EMNLP*.

Ilana Heintz, Ryan Gabbard, Mahesh Srivastava, David Barner, Donald Black, Marjorie Friedman, and Ralph Weischedel. 2013. Automatic extraction of linguistic metaphors with LDA topic modeling. In *Proc. ACL Workshop on Metaphor in NLP*.

Chaya Hiruncharoenvate, Zhiyuan Lin, and Eric Gilbert. 2015. Algorithmically bypassing censorship on sina weibo with nondeterministic homophone substitutions. In *Proc. ICWSM*.

Hongzhao Huang, Zhen Wen, Dian Yu, Heng Ji, Yizhou Sun, Jiawei Han, and He Li. 2013. Resolving entity morphs in censored data. In *Proc. ACL*.

Sanaz Jabbari, Ben Allison, and Louise Guthrie. 2008. Using a probabilistic model of context to detect word obfuscation. In *Proc. LREC*.

Gary King, Jennifer Pan, and Margaret E. Roberts. 2014. Reverse-engineering censorship in China: Randomized experimentation and participant observation. *Science*, 6199(345).

Kevin Knight and Vasileios Hatzivassiloglou. 1995. Two-level, many-paths generation. In *Proc. ACL*.

Kevin Knight, Beata Megyesi, and Christiane Schaefer. 2011. The Copiale Cipher. In *Proc. ACL Workshop on Building and Using Comparable Corpora (BUCC)*.

Irene Langkilde and Kevin Knight. 1998. Generation that exploits corpus-based statistical knowledge. In *Proc. COLING/ACL*.

Wen-Pin Lin, Matthew Snover, and Heng Ji. 2015. Unsupervised language-independent name translation mining from wikipedia infoboxes. In *Proc. EMNLP Workshop on Unsupervised Learning for NLP*.

Rada Mihalcea. 2007. Using wikipedia for automatic word sense disambiguation. In *Proc. HLT-NAACL*.

Maarten P. Mulder and Anton Nijholt. 2002. Humour research: State of the art.

Roberto Navigli. 2009. Word sense disambiguation: A survey. *ACM Computing Surveys*, 41(10).

Xiaoman Pan, Taylor Cassidy, Ulf Hermjakob, Heng Ji, and Kevin Knight. 2015. Unsupervised entity linking with abstract meaning representation. In *Proc. the 2015 Conference of the North American Chapter of the Association for Computational Linguistics —Human Language Technologies (NAACL-HLT 2015)*.

Peter Potash, Alexey Romanov, and Anna Rumshisky. 2015. Ghostwriter: Using an LSTM for automatic rap lyric generation. In *Proc. EMNLP*.

Dmitri Roussinov, Sze Wang Fong, and David Skillicorn. 2007. Detecting word substitutions: Pmi vs. hmm. In *Proc. SIGIR*.

Xing Shi, Kevin Knight, and Heng Ji. 2014. How to speak a language without knowing it. In *Proc. ACL.*

Qiudong Sun, Wenxin Ma, Wenying Yan, and Hong Dai. 2008. Text encryption technique based on robust image watermarking. *Journal of Image and Graphics.*

Pedro Szekely, Craig A Knoblock, Jason Slepicka, Andrew Philpot, Amandeep Singh, Chengye Yin, Dipsy Kapoor, Prem Natarajan, Daniel Marcu, Kevin Knight, et al. 2015. Building and using a knowledge graph to combat human trafficking. In *The Semantic Web-ISWC 2015.* Springer.

Yulia Tsvetkov. 2013. Cross-lingual metaphor detection using common semantic features. In *Proc. ACL Workshop on Metaphor in NLP.*

R. Venkateswaran and Dr V. Sundaram. 2010. Information security: Text encryption and decryption with poly substitution method and combining the features of cryptography. *International Journal of Computer Applications.*

Zhimin Wang, Houfeng Wang, Huiming Duan, Shuang Han, and Shiwen Yu. 2006. Chinese noun phrase metaphor recognition with maximum entropy approach. In *Proc. CICLING.*

David Yarowsky. 1995. Unsupervised word sense disambiguation rivaling supervised methods. In *Proc. ACL.*

Boliang Zhang, Hongzhao Huang, Xiaoman Pan, Sujian Li, Chin-Yew Lin, Heng Ji, Kevin Knight, Zhen Wen, Yizhou Sun, Jiawei Han, and Bulent Yener. 2013. Context-aware entity morph decoding. In *Proc. ACL.*

Boliang Zhang, Hongzhao Huang, Xiaoman Pan, Heng Ji, Kevin Knight, Zhen Wen, Yizhou Sun, Jiawei Han, and Bulent Yener. 2014. Be appropriate and funny: Automatic entity morph encoding. In *Proc. ACL.*

Boliang Zhang, Hongzhao Huang, Xiaoman Pan, Sujian Li, Chin-Yew Lin, Heng Ji, Kevin Knight, Zhen Wen, Yizhou Sun, Jiawei Han, and Bulent Yener. 2015. Context-aware entity morph decoding. In *Proc. ACL.*

Tao Zhu, David Phipps, Adam Pridgen, Jedidiah R. Crandall, and Dan S. Wallach. 2013. The velocity of censorship: High-fidelity detection of microblog post deletions. In *Proc. the 22nd USENIX Security Symposium.*

Author Index

Association for Computational Linguistics
209 N. Eighth Street
Stroudsburg, Pennsylvania 18360

ISBN 978-1-5108-6909-7

CURRAN ASSOCIATES INC.
proceedings.com